THE
CONCISE
LAWS
OF
HUMAN
NATURE

THE
CONCISE
LAWS
OF
HUMAN
NATURE

ROBERT GREENE

P

PROFILE BOOKS

This concise edition published in Great Britain in 2020 by
PROFILE BOOKS
29 Cloth Fair
London
EC1A 7JQ
www.profilebooks.com

Derived from *The Laws of Human Nature*, which was first published
in Great Britain in 2018 by Profile Books and in the United States of
America in 2018 by Viking, a division of Penguin Random House LLC

3 5 7 9 10 8 6 4

Printed and bound in Italy by
L.E.G.O. Spa-Lavis (TN)

A CIP catalogue record for this book is available from the British Library.

ISBN 978 1 78816 156 5
eISBN 978 1 78283 493 9

Contents

Introduction

— ✧ —

> If you come across any special trait of meanness
> or stupidity ... you must be careful not to let it
> annoy or distress you, but to look upon it merely
> as an addition to your knowledge—a new fact
> to be considered in studying the character of
> humanity. Your attitude towards it will be that
> of the mineralogist who stumbles upon a very
> characteristic specimen of a mineral.
>
> *—Arthur Schopenhauer*

Throughout the course of our lives, we inevitably have to deal with a variety of individuals who stir up trouble and make our lives difficult and unpleasant. Some of these individuals are leaders or bosses, some are colleagues, and some are friends. They can be aggressive or passive-aggressive, but they are generally masters at playing on our emotions. They often appear charming and refreshingly confident, brimming with ideas and enthusiasm, and we fall under their spell. Only when it is too late do we discover that their confidence is irrational and their ideals ill-conceived. Among colleagues, they can be those who sabotage our work or careers out of secret envy, excited to bring us down. Or they could be colleagues or hires who reveal, to our dismay, that they are completely out for themselves, using us as stepping stones.

What inevitably happens in these situations is that we are caught off guard, not expecting such behavior. Often these types will hit us with elaborate cover stories to justify their actions, or blame handy scapegoats. They know how to confuse us and draw us into a drama they control. We might protest or become angry, but in the end we feel rather helpless—the damage is done. Then another such type enters our life, and the same story repeats itself.

We often notice a similar sensation of confusion and helplessness when it comes to ourselves and our own behavior. For instance, we suddenly say something that offends our boss or colleague or friend—we are not quite sure where it came from, but we are frustrated to find that some anger and tension from within has leaked out in a way that we regret. Or perhaps we enthusiastically throw our weight into some project or scheme, only to realize it was quite foolish and a terrible waste of time. Or perhaps we fall in love with a person who is precisely the wrong type for us and we know it, but we cannot help ourselves. What has come over us, we wonder?

In these situations, we catch ourselves falling into self-destructive patterns of behavior that we cannot seem to control. It is as if we harbor a stranger within us, a little demon who operates independently of our willpower and pushes us into doing the wrong things. And this stranger within us is rather weird, or at least weirder than how we imagine ourselves.

What we can say about these two things—people's ugly actions and our own occasionally surprising behavior—is that we usually have no clue as to what causes them. We might latch onto some simple explanations: "That person is evil, a sociopath" or "Something came over me; I wasn't myself." But such pat descriptions do not lead to any understanding or prevent the same patterns from recurring. The truth is that we humans live on the surface, reacting emotionally to what people say and do. We form opinions of others and ourselves that are rather simplified. We settle for the easiest and most convenient story to tell ourselves.

What if, however, we could dive below the surface and see deep within, getting closer to the actual roots of what causes human behavior? What if we could understand why some people turn envious and try to sabotage our work, or why their misplaced confidence causes them to imagine themselves as god-like and infallible? What if we could truly fathom why people suddenly behave irrationally and reveal a much darker side to their character, or why they are always ready to provide a rationalization for their behavior, or why we continually turn to leaders who appeal to the worst in us? What if we could look deep inside and judge people's character, avoiding the bad hires and personal relationships that cause us so much emotional damage?

If we really understood the roots of human behavior, it would be much harder for the more destructive types to continually get away with their actions. We would not be so easily charmed and misled. We would be able to anticipate their nasty and manipulative maneuvers and see through their cover stories. We would not allow ourselves to get dragged into their dramas, knowing in advance that our interest is what they depend on for their control. We would finally rob them of their power through our ability to look into the depths of their character.

Similarly, with ourselves, what if we could look within and see the source of our more troubling emotions and why they drive our behavior, often against our own wishes? What if we could understand why we are so compelled to desire what other people have, or to identify so strongly with a group that we feel contempt for those who are on the outside? What if we could find out what causes us to lie about who we are, or to inadvertently push people away?

Being able to understand more clearly that stranger within us would help us to realize that it is not a stranger at all but very much a part of ourselves, and that we are far more mysterious, complex, and interesting than we had imagined. And with that awareness we would be able to break the negative patterns in our lives, stop making excuses for ourselves, and gain better control of what we do and what happens to us.

Having such clarity about ourselves and others could change the course of our lives in so many ways, but first we must clear up a common misconception: we tend to think of our behavior as largely conscious and willed. To imagine that we are not always in control of what we do is a frightening thought, *but in fact it is the reality*. We are subject to forces from deep within us that drive our behavior and that operate below the level of our awareness. We see the results—our thoughts, moods, and actions—but have little conscious access to what actually moves our emotions and compels us to behave in certain ways.

Let us call the collection of these forces that push and pull at us from deep within *human nature*. Human nature stems from the particular wiring of our brains, the configuration of our nervous system, and the way we humans process emotions, all of which developed and emerged over the course of the five million years or so of our evolution as a species. We can ascribe many of the details of our nature to the distinct way we evolved as a social animal to ensure our survival—learning to cooperate with others, coordinating our actions with the group on a high level, creating novel forms of communication and ways of maintaining group discipline. This early development lives on within us and continues to determine our behavior, even in the modern, sophisticated world we live in.

To take one example, look at the evolution of human emotion. The survival of our earliest ancestors depended on their ability to communicate with one another well before the invention of language. They evolved new and complex emotions—joy, shame, gratitude, jealousy, resentment, et cetera. The signs of these emotions could be read immediately on their faces, communicating their moods quickly and effectively. They became extremely permeable to the emotions of others as a way to bind the group more tightly together—to feel joy or grief as one—or to remain united in the face of danger.

To this day, we humans remain highly susceptible to the moods and emotions of those around us, compelling all kinds of behavior on our part—unconsciously imitating others, wanting what they have, getting swept up in viral feelings of anger or outrage. We imagine we're acting of our own free will, unaware of how deeply our susceptibility to the emotions of others in the group is affecting what we do and how we respond.

We can point to other such forces that emerged from this deep past and that similarly mold our everyday behavior—for instance, our need to continually rank ourselves and measure our self-worth through our status is a trait that is noticeable among all hunter-gatherer cultures, and even among chimpanzees, as are our tribal instincts, which cause us to divide people into insiders or outsiders. We can add to these primitive qualities our need to wear masks to disguise any behavior that is frowned upon by the tribe, leading to the formation of a shadow personality from all the dark desires we have repressed. Our ancestors understood this shadow and its dangerousness, imagining it originated from spirits and demons that needed to be exorcised. We rely on a different myth—"something came over me."

Once this primal current or force within us reaches the level of consciousness, we have to react to it, and we do so depending on our individual spirit and circumstances, usually explaining it away superficially without really understanding it. Because of the precise way in which we evolved, there are a limited number of these forces of human nature, and they lead to the behavior mentioned above—envy, grandiosity, irrationality, shortsightedness, conformity, aggression, and passive aggression, to name a few. They also lead to empathy and other positive forms of human behavior.

For thousands of years, it has been our fate to largely grope in the shadows when it comes to understanding ourselves and our own nature. We have labored under so many illusions about the human animal—imagining we descended magically from a divine source, from angels instead of primates. We have found any signs of our primitive nature and our animal roots deeply distressing, something to deny and repress. We have covered up our darker impulses with all kinds of excuses and rationalizations, making it easier for some people to get away with the most unpleasant behavior. But finally we're at a point where we can overcome our resistance to the truth about who we are through the sheer weight of knowledge we have now accumulated about human nature.

Consider *The Laws of Human Nature* a kind of codebook for deciphering people's behavior—ordinary, strange, destructive, the full gamut. Each chapter deals with a particular aspect or law of human nature. We can call them laws in that under the influence of these elemental forces, we humans tend to react in relatively predictable ways. Each chapter has ideas and strategies on how to deal with yourself and others under the influence of this law. Each chapter ends with a section on how to transform this basic human force into something more positive and productive, so that we are no longer passive slaves to human nature but actively transforming it.

You might be tempted to imagine that this knowledge is a bit old-fashioned. After all, you might argue, we are now so sophisticated and technologically advanced, so progressive and enlightened; we have moved well beyond our primitive roots; we are in the process of rewriting our nature. But the truth is in fact the opposite—we have never been more in the thrall of human nature and its destructive potential than now. And by ignoring this fact, we are playing with fire.

Look at how the permeability of our emotions has only been heightened through social media, where viral effects are continually sweeping through us and where the most manipulative leaders are able to exploit and control us. Look at the aggression that is now openly displayed in the virtual world, where it is so much easier to play out our shadow sides without repercussions. Notice how our propensities to compare ourselves with others, to feel envy, and to seek status through attention have only become intensified with our ability to communicate so quickly with so many people. And finally, look at our tribal tendencies and how they have now found the perfect medium to operate in—we can find a group to identify with, reinforce our tribal opinions in a virtual echo chamber, and demonize any outsiders, leading to mob intimidation. The potential for mayhem stemming from the primitive side of our nature has only increased.

It is simple: Human nature is stronger than any individual, than any institution or technological invention. It ends up shaping what we create to reflect itself and its primitive roots. It moves us around like pawns.

Ignore the laws at your own peril. Refusing to come to terms with human nature simply means that you are dooming yourself to patterns beyond your control and to feelings of confusion and helplessness.

The Laws of Human Nature is designed to immerse you in all aspects of human behavior and illuminate its root causes. If you let it guide you, it will radically alter how you perceive people and your entire approach to dealing with them. It will also radically change how you see yourself. It will accomplish these shifts in perspective in the following ways:

- *First, the Laws will work to transform you into a calmer and more strategic observer of people, helping to free you from all the emotional drama that needlessly drains you.*
- *Second, the Laws will make you a master interpreter of the cues that people continually emit, giving you a much greater ability to judge their character.*
- *Third, the Laws will empower you to take on and outthink the toxic types who inevitably cross your path and who tend to cause long-term emotional damage.*
- *Fourth, the Laws will teach you the true levers for*

motivating and influencing people, making your path in life that much easier.

- *Fifth, the Laws will make you realize how deeply the forces of human nature operate within you, giving you the power to alter your own negative patterns.*
- *Sixth, the Laws will transform you into a more empathetic individual, creating deeper and more satisfying bonds with the people around you.*
- *Finally, the Laws will alter how you see your own potential, making you aware of a higher, ideal self within you that you will want to bring out.*

Think of the book in the following way: you are about to become an apprentice in human nature. You will be developing some skills—how to observe and measure the character of your fellow humans and see into your own depths. You will work on bringing out your higher self. And through practice you will emerge a master of the art, able to thwart the worst that other people can throw at you and to mold yourself into a more rational, self-aware, and productive individual

> Man will only become better when you make him see what he is like.
>
> *—Anton Chekhov*

1

Master Your Emotional Self

—— ✧ ——

The Law of Irrationality

You like to imagine yourself in control of your fate, consciously planning the course of your life as best you can. But you are largely unaware of how deeply your emotions dominate you. They make you veer toward ideas that soothe your ego. They make you look for evidence that confirms what you already want to believe. They make you see what you want to see, depending on your mood, and this disconnect from reality is the source of the bad decisions and negative patterns that haunt your life. Rationality is the ability to counteract these emotional effects, to think instead of react, to open your mind to what is really happening, as opposed to what you are feeling. It does not come naturally; it is a power we must cultivate, but in doing so we realize our greatest potential.

It's just as though one's second self were standing beside one; one is sensible and rational oneself, but the other self is impelled to do something perfectly senseless, and sometimes very funny; and suddenly you notice that you are longing to do that amusing thing, goodness knows why; that is, you want to, as

it were, against your will; though you fight against
it with all of your might, you want to.

—Fyodor Dostoyevsky, A Raw Youth

Keys to Human Nature

The first step toward becoming rational is to understand
our *fundamental irrationality*. There are two factors that
should render this more palatable to our egos: nobody
is exempt from the irresistible effect of emotions on the
mind, not even the wisest among us; and to some extent
irrationality is a function of the structure of our brains
and is wired into our very nature by the way we process
emotions. Being irrational is almost beyond our control.
To understand this, we must look at the evolution of
emotions themselves.

For millions of years, living organisms depended
on finely tuned instincts for survival. In a split second,
a reptile could sense danger in the environment and
respond with an instantaneous flight from the scene.
There was no separation between impulse and action.
Then, slowly, for some animals this sensation evolved
into something larger and longer—a feeling of fear. In
the beginning this fear merely consisted of a high level
of arousal with the release of certain chemicals, alert-
ing the animal to a possible danger. With this arousal
and the attention that came with it, the animal could
respond in several ways instead of just one. It could
become more sensitive to the environment and learn.
It stood a better chance of survival because its options

were widened. This sensation of fear would last only a few seconds or even less, for speed was of the essence.

For social animals, these arousals and feelings took on a deeper and more important role: they became a critical form of communication. Vicious sounds or hair standing on end could display anger, warding off an enemy or signaling a danger; certain postures or smells revealed sexual desire and readiness; postures and gestures signaled the desire to play; certain calls from the young revealed deep anxiety and the need for the mother to return. With primates, this became ever more elaborate and complex. It has been shown that chimpanzees can feel envy and the desire for vengeance, among other emotions. This evolution took place over the course of hundreds of millions of years. Much more recently, cognitive powers developed in animals and humans, culminating in the invention of language and abstract thinking.

As many neuroscientists have affirmed, this evolution has led to the higher mammalian brain being composed of three parts. The oldest is the reptilian part of the brain, which controls all automatic responses that regulate the body. This is the instinctive part. Above that is the old mammalian or limbic brain, governing feeling and emotion. And on top of that has evolved the neocortex, the part that controls cognition and, for humans, language.

Emotions originate as physical arousal designed to capture our attention and cause us to take notice of something around us. They begin as chemical reactions and sensations that we must then translate into words to try to understand. But because they are processed in a different part of the brain from language and thinking, this translation is often slippery and inaccurate. For instance, we feel anger at person X, whereas in fact the true source of this may be envy; below the level of conscious awareness we feel inferior in relation to X and want something he or she has. But envy is not a feeling that we are ever comfortable with, and so often we translate it as something more palatable—anger, dislike, resentment.

In other words, we do not have conscious access to the originals of our emotions and the moods they generate. Once we feel them, all we can do is try to interpret the emotion, translate it into language. But more often than not we get this wrong. We latch onto interpretations that are simple and that suit us. This unconscious aspect of emotions also means that it is very hard for us to learn from them, to stop or prevent compulsive behavior.

Emotions evolved for a different reason than cognition. These two forms of relating to the world are not connected seamlessly in our brains. For animals, unburdened by the need to translate physical sensation into abstract language, emotions function smoothly, as they were meant to. For us, the split between our emotions and our cognition is a source of constant internal friction, comprising a second Emotional Self within us that operates beyond our will. Animals feel fear for a brief time, then it is gone. We dwell on our fears, intensifying them and making them last well past the moment of danger, even to the point of feeling constant anxiety.

Many might be tempted to imagine that we have somehow tamed this Emotional Self through all of our intellectual and technological progress. After all, we don't appear as violent or passionate or superstitious as our ancestors; but this is an illusion. Progress and technology have not rewired us; they have merely altered the forms of our emotions and the type of irrationality that comes with them. For instance, new forms of media have enhanced the age-old ability of politicians and others to play on our emotions, in ever subtler and more sophisticated ways. Advertisers bombard us with highly effective subliminal messages. Our continual connection to social media makes us prone to new forms of viral emotional effects. These are not media designed for calm reflection. With their constant presence, we have less and less mental space to step back and think.

Clearly the words *rational* and *irrational* can be quite loaded. People are always labeling those who disagree with them "irrational." What we need is a simple definition that can be applied as a way of judging, as accurately as possible, the difference between the two. The following shall serve as our barometer: We constantly feel emotions, and they continually infect our thinking, making us veer toward thoughts that please us and soothe our egos. It is impossible to not have our inclinations and feelings somehow involved in what we think. Rational people are aware of this and through introspection and effort are able, to some extent, to subtract emotions from their thinking and counteract their effect. Irrational people have no such awareness. They rush into action without carefully considering the ramifications and consequences.

We can see the difference in the decisions and actions that people take and the results that ensure. Rational people demonstrate over time that they are able to finish a project, to realize their goals, to work effectively with a team, and to create something that lasts. Irrational people reveal in their lives negative patterns—mistakes that keep repeating, unnecessary conflicts that follow them wherever they go, dreams and projects that are never realized, anger and desires for change that are never translated into concrete action. They are emotional and reactive and unaware of this. Everyone is capable of irrational decisions, some of which are caused by circumstances beyond our control. And even the most emotional types can hit upon great ideas or succeed momentarily through boldness. So it is important to judge over time whether a person is rational or irrational. Can they sustain success and hit upon several good strategies? Can they adjust and learn from failures?

In all cases, the degree of awareness represents the difference. Rational people can readily admit their own irrational tendencies and the need to be vigilant. On the other hand, irrational people become highly emotional when challenged about the emotional roots of their decisions. They are incapable of introspection and learning. Their mistakes make them increasingly defensive.

Fortunately, to acquire rationality is not complicated. It simply requires knowing and working through a three-step process. First, we must become aware of what we call *low-grade irrationality*. This is a function of the continual moods and feelings that we experience in life, below the level of consciousness. When we plan or make decisions, we are not aware of how deeply these moods and feelings skew the thinking process. They create in our thinking pronounced biases that are so deeply ingrained in us that we see evidence of them in all cultures and all periods of history. These biases, by distorting reality, lead to the mistakes and ineffective decisions that plague our lives. Being aware of them, we can begin to counterbalance their effects.

Second, we must understand the nature of what we shall call *high-grade irrationality*. This occurs when our emotions become inflamed, generally because of certain pressures. As we think about our anger, excitement, resentment, or suspicion, it intensifies into a reactive state—everything we see or hear is interpreted through the lens of this emotion. We become more sensitive and more prone to other emotional reactions. Impatience and resentment can bleed into anger and deep distrust. These reactive states are what lead people to violence, to manic obsessions, to uncontrollable greed, or to desires to control another person. This form of irrationality is the source of more acute problems—crises, conflicts, and disastrous decisions. Understanding how this type of irrationality operates can allow us to recognize the reactive state as it is happening and pull back before we do something we regret.

Third, we need to enact certain strategies and exercises that will strengthen the thinking part of the brain and give it more power in the eternal struggle with our emotions.

The following three steps will help you begin on the path toward rationality. It would be wise to incorporate all three into your study and practice in human nature.

Step One: Recognize the Biases

Emotions are continually affecting our thought processes and decisions, below the level of our awareness. And the most common emotion of them all is the desire for pleasure and the avoidance of pain. Our thoughts almost inevitably revolve around this desire; we simply recoil from entertaining ideas that are unpleasant or painful to us. We imagine we are looking for the truth, or being realistic, when in fact we are holding on to ideas that bring a release from tension and soothe our egos, make us feel superior. This *pleasure principle in thinking* is the source of all of our mental biases. If you believe that you are somehow immune to any of the following biases, it is simply an example of the pleasure principle in action. Instead, it is best to search and see how they continually operate inside you, as well as learn how to identify such irrationality in others.

Confirmation Bias

To hold an idea and convince ourselves we arrived at it rationally, we go in search of evidence to support our view. What could be more objective or scientific? But because of the pleasure principle and its unconscious influence, we manage to find the evidence that confirms what we *want* to believe. This is known as *confirmation bias.*

When investigating confirmation bias in the world, take a look at theories that seem a little too good to be true. Your first impulse should always be to find the evidence that disconfirms your most cherished beliefs and those of others.

Conviction Bias

We hold on to an idea that is secretly pleasing to us, but deep inside we might have some doubts as to its truth, and so we go an extra mile to convince ourselves—to believe in it with great vehemence and to loudly contradict anyone who challenges us. How can our idea not be true if it brings out in us such energy to defend it, we tell ourselves? This powerful feeling is evidence of the conviction bias at work.

Appearance Bias

We see people not as they are, but as they appear to us. And these appearances are usually misleading. First, people have trained themselves in social situations to present the front that is appropriate and that will be judged positively. Second, we are prone to fall for the *halo effect*—when we see certain negative or positive qualities in a person (social awkwardness, intelligence), other positive or negative qualities are implied that fit with this.

The Group Bias

We are social animals by nature. The feeling of isolation, of difference from the group, is depressing and terrifying. We experience tremendous relief when we find others who think the same way we do. In fact, we are motivated to take up ideas and opinions *because* they bring us this relief. We are unaware of this pull and so imagine we have come to certain ideas completely on our own.

The Blame Bias

Mistakes and failures elicit the need to explain. We want to learn the lesson and not repeat the experience. But in truth, we do not like to look too closely at what we did; our introspection is limited. Our natural response is to blame others, circumstances, or a momentary lapse of judgment. The reason for this bias is that it is often too painful to look at our mistakes.

Superiority Bias

We feel a tremendous pull to imagine ourselves as rational, decent, and ethical. These are qualities highly promoted in the culture. To shows signs otherwise is to risk great disapproval. If all of this were true—if people were rational and morally superior—the world would be suffused with goodness and peace. We know, however, the reality, and so some people, perhaps all of us, are merely deceiving ourselves. Rationality and ethical qualities must be achieved through awareness and effort. They do not come naturally. They come through a maturation process.

Step Two: Beware the Inflaming Factors

Low-grade emotions continually affect our thinking, and they originate from our own impulses—for instance, the desire for pleasing and comforting thoughts. High-grade emotion, however, comes at certain moments, reaches an explosive pitch, and is generally sparked by something external—a person who gets under our skin, or particular circumstances. The level of arousal is higher and our attention is captured completely. The more we think about the emotions, the stronger it gets, which makes us focus even more on it, and so on and so forth. Our minds tunnel into the emotion, and everything reminds us of our anger or excitement. We become reactive. Because we are unable to bear the tension this brings, high-grade emotion usually culminates in some rash action with disastrous consequences. In the middle of such an attack we feel possessed, as if a second, limbic self has taken over.

It is best to be aware of these factors so that you can stop the mind from tunneling and prevent the releasing action that you will always come to regret. You should also be aware of high-grade irrationality in others, to either get out of their way or help bring them back to reality. Here are five key inflaming factors:

Trigger Points from Early Childhood

In early childhood we were at our most sensitive and vulnerable. Our relationship to our parents had a much greater impact on us the further back in time we go. These vulnerabilities and wounds remain buried deep within our minds. Later in life, a person or event will trigger a memory of this positive or negative experience, and with it a release of powerful chemicals or hormones associated with the memory.

The way to recognize this in yourself and in others is by noticing behavior that is suddenly childish in its intensity and seemingly out of character. In the midst of such an attack, we must struggle to detach ourselves and contemplate the possible source—the wound in early childhood—and the patterns it has locked us into.

Sudden Gains or Losses

Sudden success or winnings can be very dangerous. Neurologically, chemicals are released in the brain that give a powerful jolt of arousal and energy, leading to the desire to repeat this experience. It can be the start of any kind of addiction and manic behavior.

Unexpected losses or a string of losses equally create

irrational reactions. We imagine we are cursed with bad luck and that this will go on indefinitely.

The solution here is simple: whenever you experience unusual gains or losses, that is precisely the time to step back and counterbalance them with some necessary pessimism or optimism.

Rising Pressure

Under stress or any threat, the most primitive parts of the brain are aroused and engaged, overwhelming people's reasoning powers. In fact, stress or tension can reveal flaws in people that they have carefully concealed from view. It is often wise to observe people in such moments, precisely as a way to judge their true character.

Whenever you notice rising pressure and stress levels in your life, you must watch yourself carefully. Monitor any signs of unusual brittleness or sensitivity, sudden suspicions, fears disproportionate to the circumstances. Observe with as much detachment as possible, finding time and space to be alone.

Inflaming Individuals

There are people in the world who by their nature tend to trigger powerful emotions in almost everyone they encounter. These emotions range among the extremes of love, hatred, confidence, and mistrust.

It is best to recognize these inflamers by how they affect others, not just yourself. No one can remain indifferent to them. People find themselves incapable of reasoning or maintaining any distance in their presence. They make you think of them continually when not in their presence. They have an obsessive quality, and they can lead you to extreme actions as a devoted follower or as an inveterate enemy. On either end of the spectrum—attraction or repulsion—you will tend to be irrational and you will desperately need to distance yourself. A good strategy to utilize is to see through the front they project. They inevitably try to cast a larger-than-life image; but in fact they are all too human, full of the same insecurities and weaknesses we all possess. Try to recognize these very human traits and demythologize them.

The Group Effect

This is the high-grade variety of the *group bias*. When we are in a group of a large enough size, we become different. Notice yourself and others at a sporting event, a concert, a religious or political gathering. It is impossible to not feel yourself caught up in the collective emotions.

There is an exhilarating, positive aspect to the stimulation of group emotions. But if you notice the appeal is to more diabolical emotions, such as hatred of the other, rabid patriotism, aggression, or sweeping worldviews, you need to inoculate yourself and see through the powerful pull as it works on you. It is often best to avoid the group setting if possible in order to maintain your reasoning powers, or to enter such moments with maximum skepticism.

A final word on the irrational in human nature: do not imagine that the more extreme types of irrationality have somehow been overcome through progress and enlightenment. Throughout history we witness continual cycles of rising and falling levels of the irrational. The irrational simply changes its look and its fashions.

As long as there are humans, the irrational will find its voices and means of spreading. Rationality is something to be acquired by individuals, not by mass movements or technological progress. Feeling superior and beyond it is a sure sign that the irrational is at work.

Step Three: Strategies Toward Bringing Out the Rational Self

Despite our pronounced irrational tendencies, two factors should give us all hope. First and foremost is the existence throughout history and in all cultures of people of high rationality, the types who have made progress possible. These types share certain qualities—a realistic appraisal of themselves and their weaknesses; a devotion to truth and reality; a tolerant attitude toward people; and the ability to reach goals that they have set.

The second factor is that almost all of us at some point in our lives have experienced moments of greater rationality. This often comes with what we shall call the *maker's mind-set*. We have a project to get done, perhaps with a deadline. The only emotion we can afford is excitement and energy. Other emotions simply make it impossible to concentrate. Because we have to get results, we become exceptionally practical. We focus on the work—our mind calm, our ego not intruding. If people try to interrupt or infect us with emotions, we resent it. These moments—as fleeting as a few weeks or hours—reveal the rational self that is waiting to come out. It just requires some awareness and some practice.

The following strategies are designed to help you bring out that rational self:

Know yourself thoroughly. The Emotional Self thrives on ignorance. The moment you are aware of how it operates and dominates you is the moment it loses its hold on you and can be tamed. Therefore, your first step toward the rational is always inward. You must reflect on how you operate under stress. Look at your decisions, examine your strengths, and identify what makes you different from other people.

Examine your emotions to their roots. You are angry. Let the feeling settle from within, and think about it. Was it triggered by something trivial or petty? That is a sure sign that something or someone else is behind it. Dig below any trigger points to see where they started. For these purposes, it might be wise to use a journal in which you record your self-assessments with ruthless objectivity. Find a neutral position from which you can observe your actions, with a bit of detachment and even humor.

Increase your reaction time. This power comes through practice and repetition. When some event or interaction requires a response, you must train yourself to step back. This could mean physically removing yourself to a place where you can be alone and not feel any pressure to respond. Or it could mean writing that angry email but not sending it. Cool the emotions down. The longer you take the better, because perspective comes with time.

Accept people as facts. Interactions with people are the major source of emotional turmoil, but it doesn't have to be that way. The problem is that we are continually judging people, wishing they were something that they are not. We want to change them. And because this is not possible, because everyone is different, we are continually frustrated and upset. Instead, see other people as phenomena, as neutral as comets or plants. They simply exist. Work with what they give you, instead of resisting and trying to change them. Make understanding people a fun game, the solving of puzzles. It is all part of the human comedy.

Find the optimal balance of thinking and emotion. Try to maintain a perfect balance between skepticism and curiosity. In this mode you are skeptical about your own enthusiasms and those of others. You do not accept at face value people's explanations and their application of "evidence." You look at the results of their actions, not what they say about their motivations. But if you take this too far, your mind will close itself off from wild ideas, from exciting speculations, from curiosity itself. You want to retain the elasticity of spirit you had as a child, interested in everything, while retaining the hard-nosed need to verify and scrutinize for yourself all ideas and beliefs.

Love the rational. It is important to not see the path to rationality as something painful and ascetic. In fact, it brings powers that are immensely satisfying and pleasurable, much deeper than the more manic pleasures the world tends to offer us. Being able to tame the Emotional Self leads to an overall calmness and clarity. You have the immense satisfaction of mastering yourself in a deep way.

> "Trust your feelings!"—But feelings are nothing
> final or original; behind feelings there stand
> judgments and evaluations which we inherit in the
> form of ... inclinations, aversions ... The inspiration
> born of a feeling is the grandchild of a judgement—
> and often of a false judgment!—and in any event
> not a child of your own! To trust one's feelings—
> means to give more obedience to one's grandfather
> and grandmother and their grandparents than
> to the gods which are in us: our reason and our
> experience.
>
> —*Friedrich Nietzsche*

2

Transform Self-Love into Empathy

———— ✧ ————

The Law of Narcissism

We all naturally possess the most remarkable tool for connecting to people and attaining social power–empathy. When cultivated and properly used, it can allow us to see into the moods and minds of others, giving us the power to anticipate people's actions and gently lower their resistance. This instrument, however, is blunted by our habitual self-absorption. We are all narcissists, some deeper on the spectrum than others. Our mission in life is to come to terms with this self-love and learn how to turn our sensitivity outward, toward others, instead of inward. We must recognize at the same time the toxic narcissists among us before getting enmeshed in their dramas and poisoned by their envy.

The Narcissistic Spectrum

From the moment we are born, we humans feel a never-ending need for attention. We are social animals to the core. Our survival and happiness depend on the bonds we form with others. If people do not pay attention to us, we cannot connect to them on any level. Some of this is purely physical—we must have people looking at us to feel alive. As those who have gone through long periods of isolation can attest, without eye contact we begin to doubt our existence and to descend into a deep depression. But this need is also deeply psychological: through the quality of attention we receive from others, we feel recognized and appreciated for who we are. Our sense of self-worth depends on this. Because this is so important to the human animal, people will do almost anything to get attention, including committing a crime or attempting suicide. Look behind almost any action, and you will see this need as a primary motivation.

In trying to satisfy our hunger for attention, however, we face an inevitable problem: there is only so much of it to go around. In the family, we have to compete with our siblings; at school, with classmates; at work, with colleagues. The moments in which we feel recognized and appreciated are fleeting. People can largely be indifferent to our fate, as they must deal with their own problems. There are even some who are downright hostile and disrespectful to us. How do we handle those moments when we feel psychologically alone, or even abandoned? We can double our efforts to get attention and notice, but this can exhaust our energy and it can often have the opposite effect—people who try too hard seem desperate and repulse the attention they want. We simply cannot rely on others to give us constant validation, and yet we crave it.

Facing this dilemma from early childhood on, most

of us come up with a solution that works quite well: we create a self, an image of ourselves that comforts us and makes us feel validated *from within*. This self is composed of our tastes, our opinions, how we look at the world, what we value. In building this self-image, we tend to accentuate our positive qualities and explain away our flaws. We cannot go too far in this, for if our self-image is too divorced from reality, other people will make us aware of the discrepancy, and we will doubt ourselves. But if it is done properly, in the end we have a self that we can love and cherish. Our energy turns inward. *We* become the center of our attention. When we experience those inevitable moments when we are alone or not feeling appreciated, we can retreat to this self and soothe ourselves. If we have moments of doubt and depression, our self-love raises us up, makes us feel worthy and even superior to others. This self-image operates as a thermostat, helping us to regulate our doubts and insecurities. We are no longer completely dependent on others for attention and recognition. We have *self-esteem*.

This idea might seem strange. We generally take this self-image completely for granted, like the air we breathe. It operates on a largely unconscious basis. We don't feel or see the thermostat as it operates. The best way to literally visualize this dynamic is to look at those who lack a coherent sense of self—people we shall call *deep narcissists*.

You can recognize deep narcissists by the following behavior patterns: If they are ever insulted or challenged, they have no defense, nothing internal to soothe them or validate their worth. They generally react with great rage, thirsting for vengeance, full of a sense of righteousness. This is the only way they know how to assuage their insecurities. In such battles, they will position themselves as the wounded victim, confusing others and even drawing sympathy. They are prickly and oversensitive. Almost everything is taken personally. They can become quite paranoid and have enemies in all directions to point to. You can see an impatient or distant look on their face whenever you talk about something that does not directly involve them in some way. They immediately turn the conversation back to themselves, with some story or anecdote to distract from the insecurity behind it. They can be prone to vicious bouts of envy if they see others getting the attention they feel they deserve. They frequently display extreme self-confidence. This always helps to gain attention, and it neatly covers up their gaping inner emptiness and their fragmented sense of self. But beware if this confidence is ever truly put to the test.

Let us imagine narcissism as a way of gauging the level of our self-absorption, as if it existed on a measurable scale from high to low. At a certain depth, let us say below the halfway mark on the scale, people enter the realm of deep narcissism. Once they reach this depth, it is very difficult for them to raise themselves back up, because they lack the self-esteem device. The deep narcissist becomes completely self-absorbed, almost always below the mark. If for a moment they manage to engage with others, some comment or action will trigger their insecurities and they will go plummeting down. But mostly they tend to sink deeper into themselves over time. Other people are instruments. Reality is just a reflection of their needs. Constant attention is their only way of survival.

Above that halfway mark is what we shall call the *functional narcissist*, where most of us reside. We also are self-absorbed, but what prevents us from falling deep into ourselves is a coherent sense of self that we can rely upon and love. This creates some inner resiliency. We may have deeper narcissistic moments, fluctuating below the mark, particularly when depressed or challenged in life, but inevitably we elevate ourselves. Not feeling continually insecure or wounded, not always needing to fish for attention, functional narcissists can turn their attention outward, into their work and into building relationships with people.

Our task, as students of human nature, is threefold. First, we must fully understand the phenomenon of the deep narcissist. Although they are in the minority, some of them can inflict an unusual amount of harm in the world. We must be able to distinguish the toxic types that stir up drama and try to turn us into objects they can use for their purposes. They can draw us in with their unusual energy, but if we become enmeshed, it can be a nightmare to disengage. They are masters at turning the tables and making others feel guilty. Narcissistic leaders are the most dangerous of all, and we must resist their pull and see through the façade of their apparent creativity. Knowing how to handle the deep narcissists in our lives is an important art for all of us.

Second, we must be honest about our own nature and not deny it. We are all narcissists. In a conversation we are all champing at the bit to talk, to tell our story, to give our opinion. We like people who share our ideas—they reflect back to us our good taste. If we happen to be assertive, we see assertiveness as a positive quality because it is ours, whereas others, more timid, will rate it as obnoxious and value introspective qualities. We are all prone to flattery because of our self-love. Moralizers who try to separate themselves and denounce the narcissists in the world today are often the biggest narcissists of them all—they love the sound of their voice as they point fingers and preach. *We are all on the spectrum of self-absorption.* Creating a self that we can love is a healthy development, and there should be no stigma attached to it. Without self-esteem from within, we would fall into deep narcissism. But to move beyond functional narcissism, which should be our goal, we must first be honest with ourselves. Trying to deny our self-absorbed nature, trying to pretend we are somehow more altruistic than others, makes it impossible for us to transform ourselves.

Third and most important, we must begin to make the transformation into the *healthy narcissist*. Healthy narcissists have a stronger, even more resilient sense of self. They tend to hover closer to the top of the scale. They recover more quickly from any wounds or insults. They do not need as much validation from others. They realize at some point in life that they have limits and flaws. They can laugh at these flaws and not take slights so personally. In many ways, by embracing the full picture of themselves, their self-love is more real and complete. From this stronger inner position, they can turn their attention outward more often and more easily. This attention goes in one of two directions, and sometimes both. First, they are able to direct their focus and their love into their work, becoming great artists, creators, and inventors. Because their outward focus on the work is more intense, they tend to be successful in their ventures, which gives them the necessary attention and validation. They can have moments of doubt and insecurity, and artists can be notoriously brittle, but work stands as a continual release from too much self-absorption.

The other direction healthy narcissists take is toward people, developing empathic powers. Imagine empathy as the realm lying at the very top of the scale and beyond—complete absorption in others. By our very nature, we humans have tremendous abilities to understand people from the inside out. In our earliest years we felt completely bonded with our mother, and we could sense her every mood and read her every emotion in a preverbal way. Unlike any other animal or primate, we also had the ability to extend this beyond the mother to other caregivers and people in our vicinity.

This is the physical form of empathy that we feel even to this day with our closest friends, spouses, or partners. We also have a natural ability to take the perspective of others, to think our way inside their minds. These powers largely lie dormant because of our self-absorption. But in our twenties and beyond, feeling more confident about ourselves, we can begin to focus outward, on people, and rediscover these powers. Those who practice this empathy often become superior social observers in the arts or sciences, therapists, and leaders of the highest order.

Our brains were built for continual social interaction; the complexity of this interaction is one of the main factors that drastically increased our intelligence as a species. At a certain point, involving ourselves less with others has a net negative effect on the brain itself and atrophies our social muscle. To make matters worse, our culture tends to emphasize the supreme value of the individual and individual rights, encouraging greater self-involvement. We find more and more people who cannot imagine that others have a different perspective, that we are all not exactly the same in what we desire or think.

You must try to run counter to these developments and create empathic energy. Each side of the spectrum has its peculiar momentum. Deep narcissism tends to sink you deeper, as your connection to reality lessens and you are unable to really develop your work or your relationships. Empathy does the opposite. As you increasingly turn your attention outward, you get constant positive feedback. People want to be around you more. You develop your empathic muscle; your work improves; without trying, you gain the attention that humans thrive on. Empathy creates its own upward, positive momentum.

The following are the four components that go into the empathic skill set.

The empathic attitude: Empathy is more than anything a state of mind, a different way of relating to others. The greatest danger you face is your general assumption that you really understand people and that you can quickly judge and categorize them. Instead, you must begin with the assumption that you are ignorant and that you have natural biases that will make you judge people incorrectly. The people around you present a mask that suits their purposes. You mistake the mask for reality. Let go of your tendency to make snap judgements. Open your mind to seeing people in a new light. Do not assume that you are similar or that they share your values. Each person you meet is like an undiscovered country, with a very particular psychological chemistry that you will carefully explore. You are more than ready to be surprised by what you uncover. This flexible, open spirit is similar to creative energy—a willingness to consider more possibilities and options. In fact, developing your empathy will improve your creative powers.

Visceral empathy: Empathy is an instrument of emotional attunement. It is hard for us to read or figure out the thoughts of another person, but feelings and moods are much easier for us to pick up. We are all prone to catching the emotions of another person. The physical boundaries between us and other people are much more permeable than we realize. People are continually affecting our moods. What you are doing here is turning this physiological response into knowledge. Pay deep attention to the moods of people, as indicated by their body language and tone of voice. When they talk, they have a feeling tone that is either in sync or not in sync with what they are saying. This tone can be one of confidence, insecurity, defensiveness, arrogance, frustration, elation. This tone manifests itself physically in their voice, their gestures, and their posture. In each encounter, you must try to detect this before even paying attention to what they are saying. This will register to you viscerally, in your own physical response to them. A defensive tone on their part will tend to create a like feeling in you.

Analytic empathy: The reason you are able to understand your friends or partner so deeply is that you have a lot of information about their tastes, values, and family background. We have all had the experience of thinking we know someone but over time having to adjust our original impression once we get more information. So while physical empathy is extremely powerful, it must be supplemented by analytic empathy. This can prove particularly helpful with people toward whom we feel resistant and whom we have a hard time identifying with—either because they are very different from us or because there is something about them that repels us. In such cases we naturally resort to judging and putting them into categories. There are people out there who are not worth the effort—supreme fools or true psychopaths. But for most others who seem hard to figure out, we should see it as an excellent challenge and a way to improve our skills. As Abraham Lincoln said, "I don't like that man. I must get to know him better."

The empathic skill: Becoming empathetic involves a process, like anything. In order to make sure that you are really making progress and improving your ability to understand people on a deeper level, you need feedback. This can come in one of two forms: direct and indirect. In the direct form, you ask people about their thoughts and feelings to get a sense of whether you have guessed correctly. This must be discreet and based on a level of trust, but it can be a very accurate gauge of your skill. Then there is the indirect form—you sense a greater rapport and how certain techniques have worked for you.

> The deepest principle of Human Nature is the craving to be appreciated.
>
> *—William James*

Three Examples of Narcissistic Types

The Complete Control Narcissist. The great riddle that the Complete Control type presents is how people who are so deeply narcissistic can also be so charming and, through their charm, gain influence. How can they possibly connect with others when they are so clearly self-obsessed? How are they able to mesmerize? The answer lies in the early part of their careers, before they turn paranoid and vicious.

These types generally have more ambition and energy than the average deep narcissist. They also tend to have even greater insecurities. The only way they can mollify these insecurities and satisfy their ambition is by gaining from others more than the usual share of attention and validation, which can really only come through securing social power in either politics or business. Early on in life, these types stumble upon the best means for doing so. As with most deep narcissists, they are hypersensitive to any perceived slight. They have fine antennae attuned to people to probe their feelings and thoughts—to suss out if there is any hint of disrespect. But what they discover at some point is that this sensitivity can be tuned to others to probe *their* desires and insecurities. Being so sensitive, they can listen to people with deep attention. They can mimic empathy. The difference is that from within, they are impelled not by the need to connect but by the need to control people and manipulate them. They listen and probe you in order to discover weaknesses to play on.

The Theatrical Narcissist. One of the strange paradoxes about deep narcissism is that it often goes unnoticed by others, until the behavior becomes too extreme to ignore. The reason for this is simple: deep narcissists can be masters of disguise. They sense early on that if they revealed their true selves to others—their need for constant attention and to feel superior—they would repel people. They use their lack of a coherent self as an advantage. They can play many parts. They can disguise their need for attention through various dramatic devices. They can go further than anyone in seeming moral and altruistic. They never just give or support the right cause—*they make a show of it*. Who wants to doubt the sincerity of this display of morality? Or they go in the opposite direction, reveling in their status as a victim, as someone suffering at the hands of others or neglected by the world. It is easy to get caught up in the drama of the moment, only to suffer later as they consume you with their needs or use you for their purposes. They play on *your* empathy.

Your only solution is to see through the trick. Recognize this type by the fact that the focus always seems to be on them. Notice how they are always superior in supposed goodness or suffering or squalor. See the continual drama and the theatrical quality of their gestures. Everything they do or say is for public consumption. Do not let yourself become collateral damage in their drama.

The Healthy Narcissist—the Mood Reader. Leaders infect the group with their mind-set. Much of this occurs on the nonverbal level, as people pick up on the leader's body language and tone of voice. A healthy narcissist imbues himself with an air of complete confidence and optimism and watches how this infects his team's spirit. A strong leader also has to divide his attention almost equally between individuals and the group. If he notices a particular mood among his team, he should try to anticipate what they might do by putting himself in a similar mood. Finally, in detecting any dips in spirit or negativity, the healthy narcissist must be gentle. Scolding will only make people feel ashamed and singled out, which would lead to contagious effects down the road. Better to engage them in talk, to enter their spirit, and to find indirect ways to either elevate their mood or isolate them without making them realize what he is doing.

What makes us develop these empathic powers is necessity. If we feel our survival depends on how well we gauge the moods and minds of others, then we will find the requisite focus and tap into the powers. The first step to developing these powers is to realize you have a remarkable social tool that you are not cultivating. The best way to see this is to try it out. Stop your incessant interior monologue and pay deeper attention to people. Attune yourself to the shifting moods of individuals and the group. Get a read on each person's particular psychology and what motivates them. Try to take their perspective, enter their world and value system. You will suddenly become aware of an entire world of nonverbal behavior you never knew existed.

> I do not ask the wounded person how he feels ... I myself become the wounded person.
>
> —*Walt Whitman*

3

See Through People's Masks

—— ✧ ——

The Law of Role-playing

People tend to wear the mask that shows them off in the best possible light–humble, confident, diligent. They say the right things, smile, and seem interested in our ideas. They learn to conceal their insecurities and envy. If we take this appearance for reality, we never really know their true feelings, and on occasion we are blindsided by their sudden resistance, hostility, and manipulative actions. Fortunately, the mask has cracks in it. People continually leak out their true feelings and unconscious desires in the nonverbal cues they cannot completely control–facial expressions, vocal inflections, tension in the body, and nervous gestures. You must master this language by transforming yourself into a superior reader of men and women. Armed with this knowledge, you can take the proper defensive measures. On the other hand, since appearances are what people judge you by, you must learn how to present the best front and play your role to maximum effect.

You will always be the prey or the plaything of
the devils and fools in this world, if you expect to

see them going about with horns or jangling their bells. And it should be borne in mind that, in their intercourse with others, people are like the moon: they show you only one of their sides. Every man has an innate talent for ... making a mask out of his physiognomy, so that he can always look as if he really were what he pretends to be ... and its effect is extremely deceptive. He dons his mask whenever his object is to flatter himself into some one's good opinion; and you may pay just as much attention to it as if it were made of wax or cardboard.

—Arthur Schopenhauer

Keys to Human Nature

We humans are consummate actors. We learn at an early age how to get what we want from our parents by putting on certain looks that will elicit sympathy or affection. We learn how to conceal from our parents or siblings exactly what we're thinking or feeling, to protect ourselves in vulnerable moments. We become good at flattering those whom it is important to win over—popular peers or teachers. We learn how to fit into the group by wearing the same clothes and speaking the same language. As we get older and strive to carve out a career, we learn how to create the proper front in order to be hired and to fit into a group culture. If we become an executive or a professor or a bartender, we must act the part.

Although we are all expert actors, at the same

time we secretly experience this need to act and play a part as a burden. We are the most successful social animal on the planet. For hundreds of thousands of years our hunter-gatherer ancestors could survive only by constantly communicating with one another through non-verbal cues. Developed over so much time, before the invention of language, that is how the human face became so expressive, and gestures so elaborate. This is bred deep within us. We have a continual desire to communicate our feelings and yet at the same time the need to conceal them for proper social functioning. With these counterforces battling inside us, we cannot completely control what we communicate. Our real feelings continually leak out in the form of gestures, tones of voice, facial expressions, and posture. We are not trained, however, to pay attention to people's nonverbal cues. By sheer habit, we fixate on the words people say, while also thinking about what we'll say next. What this means is that we are using only a small percentage of the potential social skills we all possess.

Your task as a student of human nature is twofold: First, you must understand and accept the theatrical quality of life. You do not moralize and rail against the role-playing and the wearing of masks so essential to smooth social functioning. In fact, your goal is to play your part on the stage of life with consummate skill, attracting attention, dominating the limelight, and making yourself into a sympathetic hero or heroine. Second, you must not be naïve and mistake people's appearances for reality. You are not blinded by people's acting skills.

You transform yourself into a master decoder of their true feelings, working on your observation skills and practicing them as much as you can in daily life.

And so, for these purposes, there are three aspects to this particular law: understanding *how* to observe people; learning some basic keys for decoding nonverbal communication; and mastering the art of what is known as *impression management*, playing your role to maximum effect.

Observational Skills

As with any skill, this will require patience. What you are doing is slowly rewiring your brain through practice, mapping new neuronal connections. You do not want to overload yourself in the beginning with too much information. You need to take baby steps, to see small but daily progress. In a casual conversation with someone, give yourself the goal of observing one or two facial expressions that seem to go against what the person is saying or indicate some additional information. Be attentive to microexpressions, quick flashes on the face of tension, or forced smiles. Once you succeed in this simple exercise with one person, try it with someone else, always focusing on the face. Once you find it easier to notice cues from the face, attempt to make a similar observation about an individual's voice, noting any changes in pitch or the pace of talking. The voice says a lot about people's level of confidence and their contentment. Later on graduate to elements of body language—such as posture, hand gestures, positioning of legs. Keep these exercises simple, having simple goals. Write down any observations, particularly any patterns you notice.

As you practice these exercises, you must be relaxed and open to what you see, not champing at the bit to interpret your observations with words. You must be engaged in the conversation while talking less and trying to get them to talk more. Try to mirror them, making comments that play off something they have said and reveal you are listening to them. This will have the effect of making them relax and want to talk more, which will make them leak out more nonverbal cues. But your observing of people must never be obvious. Feeling scrutinized, people will freeze up and try to control their expressions. Too much direct eye contact will betray you. You must appear natural and attentive, using only quick peripheral glances to notice any changes in the face, voice, or body.

In observing any particular individual over time, you need to establish their baseline expression and mood. Aware of a person's usual demeanor you can pay greater attention to any deviations—for instance, sudden animation in someone who is generally reserved, or a relaxed look from the habitually nervous. Once you know a person's baseline, it will be much easier to see signs of dissimulation or distress in them. Related to the baseline expression, try to observe the same person in different settings, noticing how their nonverbal cues change if they are talking to a spouse, a boss, an employee.

In practicing this skill you must be aware of some common errors you can fall into. If you are not careful, you will glean signs but quickly interpret them to fit your own emotional biases about people, which will make your observations not only useless but also dangerous. If you are observing someone you naturally dislike, or who reminds you of someone unpleasant in your past, you will tend to see almost any cue as unfriendly or hostile. You will do the opposite for people you like. In these exercises you must strive to subtract your personal preferences and prejudices about people.

As part of your practice, try to observe yourself as well. Notice how often and when you tend to put on a fake smile, or how your body registers nervousness—in your voice, the drumming of your fingers, the twiddling with your hair, the quivering of your lips, and so on. Becoming acutely aware of your own nonverbal behavior will make you more sensitive and alert to the signals of others. You will be better able to imagine the emotions that go with the cue. And you will also gain greater control of your nonverbal behavior, something very valuable for playing the right social role.

Finally, in developing these observational skills you will notice a physical change in yourself and in your relation to people. You will become increasingly sensitive to people's shifting moods and even anticipate them as you feel inside something of what they're feeling. Taken far enough, such powers can make you seem almost psychic.

Decoding Keys

Remember that people are generally trying to present the best possible front to the world. This means concealing their possible antagonistic feelings, their desires for power or superiority, their attempts at ingratiation, and their insecurities. Your task is to look past the distractions and become aware of those signs that leak out automatically, revealing something of the true emotion beneath the mask. The three categories of the most important cues to observe and identify are *dislike/like, dominance/submission,* and *deception.*

Dislike/like cues: People give out clear indications in their body language of active dislike or hostility. These include the sudden squinting of the eyes at something you have said, the glare, the pursing of the lips until they nearly disappear, the stiff neck, the torso or feet that turn away from you while you are still engaged in a conversation, the folding of the arms as you try to make a point, and an overall tenseness in the body. The problem is that you will not usually see such signs unless a person's displeasure has become too strong to conceal. Instead, you must train yourself to look for the microexpressions and the other more subtle signs that people give out.

The microexpression is a recent discovery among psychologists who have been able to document its existence through film. It lasts less than a second. These expressions will be a momentary glare, tensing of the facial muscles, pursing of the lips, the beginnings of a frown or sneer or look of contempt, with the eyes looking down. Once you begin to notice such expressions, you will find it easier to catch them.

People will often give themselves away with the mixed signal—a positive comment to distract you but some clearly negative body language. Pay attention as well to the opposite configuration—someone says something sarcastic and pointed, directed at you, but they do this with a smile and a jokey tone of voice, as if to signal it is all in good humor. It is their repressed way of expressing their hostility. Take notice of people who praise or flatter you without their eyes lighting up. This could be a sign of hidden envy.

On the other side of the coin, we generally have less of a need to hide positive emotions from others, but nonetheless we often do not like to emit obvious signs of joy and attraction, especially in work situations, or even in courtship. People often prefer to display a cool social front. So there is great value in being able to detect the signs that people are falling under your spell.

People who feel positive emotions for you will display noticeable signs of relaxation in the facial muscles, particularly in the lines of the forehead and the area around the mouth; their lips will appear more fully exposed and the whole area around their eyes will widen. These are all involuntary expressions of comfort and openness.

In developing your skills in this arena, you must learn to distinguish between the fake and genuine smile.

Because the genuine variety is less common, you must know how to recognize it. The genuine smile will affect the muscles around the eyes and widen them, often revealing crow's-feet on the side of the eyes. It will also tend to pull the cheeks upward. There is no genuine smile without a definite change in the eyes and cheeks.

Perhaps the most telling indication of positive emotions comes from the voice. When people are engaged and excited to talk to you, the pitch of their voice rises, indicating emotional arousal.

Finally, monitoring nonverbal cues is essential in your attempts at influencing and seducing people. When people start to feel comfortable in your presence, they will stand closer to you or lean in, nodding, their arms not folded or revealing any tension. Perhaps the best and most exciting sign of all is synchrony, the other person unconsciously mirroring you.

Dominance/submission cues: People's actions will often contain dominance and submission cues. For instance, people will often show up late to indicate their superiority, real or imagined. They are not obligated to be on time. Also, conversation patterns reveal the relative position people feel they occupy. For instance, those who feel dominant will tend to talk more and interrupt frequently, as a means of asserting themselves. When there's an argument that turns personal, they will resort to what is known as punctuation—they will find an action on the other side that started it all, even though clearly it is part of the relationship pattern. They assert their interpretation of who is to blame through their tone of voice and piercing looks. If you observe a couple from the outside, you will frequently notice one person who is in the dominant position. If you converse with them, the dominant one will make eye contact with you but not with his or her partner, and will appear to only half listen to what the partner says. Smiles can also be a subtle cue for indicating superiority, especially through what we shall call the tight smile. This usually comes in response to something someone said, and it is a smile that tightens the facial muscles and indicates irony and contempt for the person they see as inferior but gives them the cover of appearing friendly.

One final but very subtle nonverbal means of asserting dominance in a relationship comes through the *symptom*. One partner suddenly develops headaches or some other illness, or starts drinking, or generally falls into a negative pattern of behavior. This forces the other side to play by the rules, to tend to their weakness. It is the willful use of sympathy to gain power and it is extremely effective.

Finally, use the knowledge you glean from these cues as a valuable means of gauging the levels of confidence in people and acting appropriately. With leaders who are riddled with insecurities that poke through nonverbally, you can play to their insecurities and gain power through this, but often it is best to avoid attaching yourself too closely to such types as they tend to do poorly over time and can drag you down with them. With those who are not leaders but are trying to assert themselves as if they were, your response should depend on their personality type. If they are rising stars, full of self-belief and a sense of destiny, it might be wise to try to rise with them. You will notice such types by the positive energy that surrounds them. On the other hand, if they are simply arrogant and petty despots, these are precisely the types you should always strive to avoid, as they are masters at making others pay lip service to them without giving anything in return.

Deception cues: The most clear and common sign of deception comes when people assume an extra-animated front. When they smile a lot, seem more than friendly and even are quite entertaining, it is hard for us to not be drawn in and lower ever so slightly our resistance to their influence. Similarly, if people are trying to cover something up, they tend to become extra vehement, righteous, and chatty. With such deceivers you will often notice that one part of the face or the body is more expressive to attract your attention. This will often be the area around the mouth, with large smiles and changing expressions. This is the easiest area of the body for people to manipulate and create an animated effect. But it could also be exaggerated gestures with the hands and arms. The key is that you will detect tension and anxiety in other parts of the body, because it is impossible for them to control all of the muscles. When they flash a big smile, the eyes are tense with little movement or the rest of the body is unusually still, or if the eyes are trying to fool you with looks to garner your sympathy, the mouth quivers slightly. These are signs of contrived behavior, of trying too hard to control one part of the body.

In general, the best thing to do when you suspect people of trying to distract you from the truth is not to actively confront them in the beginning, but in fact to encourage them to continue by showing interest in what they are saying or doing. You want them to talk more, to reveal more signs of tension and contrivance. At the right moment you must surprise them with a question or remark that is designed to make them uncomfortable, revealing you are onto them. Pay attention to the microexpressions and body language they emit at such moments. If they are really deceiving, they will often have a freeze response as they take this in, and then quickly try to mask the underlying anxiety.

Even with the most practiced deceivers, one of the best ways to unmask them is to notice how they give emphasis to their words through nonverbal cues. Emphasis comes through raised vocal pitch and assertive tone, forceful hand gestures, the raising of eyebrows and the widening of eyes. We engage in such behavior when we are filled with emotion and trying to add an exclamation point to what we are saying. It is hard for deceivers to mimic this.

Finally, with deception keep in mind that there is always a scale involved. At the bottom of the scale we find the most harmless varieties, little white lies. It is best to simply ignore this lower end. Polite, civilized society depends on the ability to say things that are not always sincere. Save your alertness for those situations in which the stakes are higher and people might be angling to get something valuable out of you.

The Art of Impression Management

Consciously or unconsciously most of us adhere to what is expected of our role because we realize our social success depends on this. Some may refuse to play this game, but in the end they are marginalized and forced to play the outsider role, with limited options and decreasing freedom as they get older. In general, it is best to simply accept this dynamic and derive some pleasure from it. You are not only aware of the proper appearances you must present but know how to shape them for maximum effect. You can then transform yourself into a superior actor on the stage of life and enjoy your moment in the limelight.

The following are some basics in the art of impression management.

Master the nonverbal cues. In certain settings, when people want to get a fix on who we are, they pay greater attention to the nonverbal cues we emit. Aware of this, smart social performers will know how to control these cues to some degree and consciously emit the signs that are suitable and positive. They know how to seem likable, flash genuine smiles, use welcoming body language, and mirror the people they deal with. In general, you want to be aware of your nonverbal style so you can consciously alter certain aspects for better effect.

Be a method actor. In method acting you train yourself to be able to display the proper emotions on command. You feel sad when your part calls for it by recalling your experiences that caused such emotions, or if necessary by simply imagining such experiences. Learn how to consciously put yourself in the right emotional mood by imagining how and why you should feel the emotion suitable to the occasion or performance you are about to give. Surrender to the feeling for the moment so that the face and body are naturally animated. Just as important, train yourself to return to a more neutral expression at a natural moment, careful to not go too far with your emoting.

Adapt to your audience. Although you conform to certain parameters set by the role you play, you must be flexible. Know your audience and shape your nonverbal cues to their style and taste.

Create the proper first impression. You must give extra attention to your first appearance before an individual or group. In general it is best to tone down your nonverbal cues and present a more neutral front. A relaxed smile, however, and looking people in the eye in these first encounters can do wonders for lowering their natural resistance.

Use dramatic effects. You must know how to selectively absent yourself, to regulate how often and when you appear before others making them want to see more of you, not less. Learn to withhold information. In general, make your appearances and your behavior less predictable.

Project saintly qualities. You will want to be seen giving generously to certain causes and supporting them on social media. Projecting sincerity and honesty always plays well. A few public confessions of your weaknesses and vulnerabilities will do the trick. Learn how to occasionally lower your head and appear humble. If dirty work must be done, get others to do it. Your hands are clean. Never overtly play the Machiavellian leader—that only works well on television. Use the appropriate dominance cues to make people think you are powerful, even before you reach the heights. You want to seem like you were *destined* for success, a mystical effect that always works.

> "You appeared to read a good deal upon her
> which was quite invisible to me." "Not invisible
> but unnoticed, Watson. You did not know where
> to look, and so you missed all that was important.
> I can never bring you to realize the importance of
> sleeves, the suggestiveness of thumbnails, or the
> great issues that may hang from a boot-lace."
> –*Sir Arthur Conan Doyle, "A Case of Identity"*

4

Determine the Strength
of People's Character

— ✧ —

The Law of Compulsive Behavior

*When choosing people to work and associate with, do not be
mesmerized by their reputation or taken in by the surface image
they try to project. Instead, train yourself to look deep within
them and see their character. People's character is formed in
their earliest years and by their daily habits. It is what compels
them to repeat certain actions in their lives and fall into negative patterns. Look closely at such patterns and remember that
people never do something just once. They will inevitably repeat
their behavior. Gauge the relative strength of their character
by how well they handle adversity, their ability to adapt and
work with other people, their patience and ability to learn. Always gravitate toward those who display signs of strength, and
avoid the many toxic types out there. Know thoroughly your own
character so you can break your compulsive patterns and take
control of your destiny.*

Character is destiny.

—*Heraclitus*

Keys to Human Nature

If we are honest with ourselves, we must admit there is some truth to the concept of fate. We are prone to repeat the same decisions and methods of dealing with problems. There is a pattern to our life, particularly visible in our mistakes and failures. But there is a different way of looking at this concept: it is not spirits or gods that control us but rather our *character*. The etymology of the word *character*, from the ancient Greek, refers to an engraving or stamping instrument. Character, then, is something that is so deeply ingrained or stamped within us that it compels us to act in certain ways, beyond our awareness and control.

As a student of human nature your task is twofold: First you must come to understand your own character, examining as best you can the elements in your past that have gone into forming it, and the patterns, mostly negative, that you can see recurring in your life. It is impossible to get rid of this stamp that constitutes your character. It is too deep. But through awareness, you can learn to mitigate or stop certain negative patterns. You can work to transform the negative and weak aspects of your character into actual strengths. You can try to create new habits and patterns that go with them through practice, actively shaping your character and the destiny that goes with it.

Second, you must develop your skill in reading the character of the people you deal with. To do so, you must consider character as a primary value when it comes to choosing a person to work for or with or an intimate partner. This means giving it more value than their charm, intelligence, or reputation. The ability to observe people's character—as seen in their actions and patterns—is an absolutely critical social skill. It can help you avoid precisely those kinds of decisions that can spell years of misery—choosing an incompetent leader, a shady partner, a scheming assistant, or the kind of incompatible spouse who can poison your life. But it is a skill you must consciously develop, because we humans are generally inept when it comes to such assessments.

The general source of our ineptness is that we tend to base our judgments of people on what is most apparent. But people often try to cover up their weaknesses by presenting them as something positive.

The first step, then, in studying character is to be aware of these illusions and facades and to train ourselves to look through them. We must scrutinize everybody for signs of their character, no matter the appearance they present or the position they occupy. With this firmly in mind, we can then work on several key components to the skill: recognizing certain signs that people emit in certain situations and that clearly reveal their character; understanding some general categories that people fit into (strong versus weak character, for instance), and finally being aware of certain types of characters that often are the most toxic and should be avoided if possible.

Character Signs

The most significant indicator of people's character comes through their actions over time. Despite what people say about the lessons they have learned, and how they have changed over the years, you will inevitably notice the same actions and decisions repeating in the course of their life. In these decisions they reveal their character. You must take notice of any salient forms of behavior—disappearing when there is too much stress, not completing an important piece of work, turning suddenly belligerent when challenged, or, conversely, suddenly rising to the occasion when given responsibility. With this fixed in your mind, you do some research into their past. You look at other actions you have observed that fit into this pattern, now in retrospect. You pay close attention to what they do in the present. You see their actions not as isolated incidents but as parts of a compulsive pattern. If you ignore the pattern it is your own fault.

You must always keep in mind the primary corollary of this law: people never do something just once. They might try to excuse themselves, to say they lost their heads in the moment, but you can be sure they will repeat whatever foolishness they did on another occasion, compelled by their character and habits. In fact, they will often repeat actions when it is completely against their self-interest, revealing the compulsive nature of their weaknesses.

It is critical that you measure the relative strength of

people's character. Think of it in this way: such strength comes from deep within the core of the person. It could stem from a mixture of certain factors—genetics, secure parenting, good mentors along the way, and constant improvement. Whatever the cause, this strength is not something displayed on the outside in the form of bluster or aggression but manifests itself in overall resilience and adaptability. Strong character has a tensile quality like a good piece of metal—it can give and bend but still retains its overall shape and never breaks.

The strength emanates from a feeling of personal security and self-worth. This allows such people to take criticism and learn from their experiences. This means they do not give up so easily, since they want to learn how to get better. They are rigorously persistent. People of strong character are open to new ideas and ways of doing things without compromising the basic principles they adhere to. People of weak character begin from the opposite position. They are easily overwhelmed by circumstances, making them hard to rely upon. They are slippery and evasive. Worst of all, they cannot be taught because learning from others implies criticism. This means you will continually hit a wall in dealing with them. They may appear to listen to your instructions, but they will simply revert to what they think is best.

We are all a mix of strong and weak qualities, but some people clearly veer in one or the other direction. As much as you can, you want to work and associate with strong characters and avoid weak ones.

In gauging strength or weakness, look at how people

handle stressful moments and responsibility. Look at their patterns: what have they actually completed or accomplished? You can also test people. For instance, a good-natured joke at their expense can be quite revealing. Do they respond graciously to this, not so easily caught up in their insecurities, or do their eyes flash resentment or even anger? To gauge their trustworthiness as a team player, give them strategic information or share with them some rumor—do they quickly pass along the information to others? Are they quick to take one of your ideas and package it as their own? Criticize them in a direct manner. Do they take this to heart and try to learn and improve, or do they show overt signs of resentment? Give them an open-ended assignment with less direction than usual and monitor how they organize their thoughts and their time. Challenge them with a difficult assignment or some novel way of doing something, and see how they respond, how they handle their anxiety.

Remember: weak character will neutralize all of the other possible good qualities a person might possess. There are hidden costs to working with them or hiring them. Someone less charming and intelligent but of strong character will prove more reliable and productive over the long run. People of real strength are as rare as gold, and if you find them, you should respond as if you had discovered a treasure.

Toxic Types

Although each person's character is as unique as a fingerprint, we can notice throughout history certain types that keep recurring and that can be particularly pernicious to deal with. As opposed to the more obviously evil or manipulative characters that you can spot a mile away, these types are trickier. Only over time do you see the toxic nature beneath the appearance, often when it is too late. Your best defense is to be armed with knowledge of these types, to notice the signs earlier on, and to not get involved or to disengage from them as quickly as possible.

The Hyperperfectionist: You are lured into their circle by how hard they work, how dedicated they are to making the best of whatever it is they produce. But if you have the misfortune of agreeing to work with or for such a type, you will slowly discover the reality. They cannot delegate tasks; they have to oversee everything. It is less about high standards and dedication to the group than about power and control.

Such people often have dependency issues stemming from their family background. Any feeling that they might have to depend on someone for something opens up old wounds and anxieties. They have patterns of initial success followed by burnout and spectacular failures. It is best to recognize the type before getting enmeshed on any level.

The Relentless Rebel: They hate authority and love the underdog. These types will often have a biting sense of humor, which they might turn on you, but that is part of their authenticity, their need to deflate everyone, or so you think. But if you happen to associate with this type more closely, you will see that it is something they cannot control; it is a compulsion to feel superior, not some higher moral quality.

In their childhood a parent or father figure probably disappointed them. They came to mistrust and hate all those in power. In the end, they cannot accept any criticism from others because that reeks of authority. Such types are eternally locked in adolescence, and to try work with them will prove as productive as trying to lock horns with a sullen teenager.

The Personalizer: These people seem so sensitive and thoughtful, a rare and nice quality. What you come to realize later on is that their sensitivity really only goes in one direction—inward. They are prone to take *everything* that people say or do as personal. As children, they had a gnawing feeling that they never got enough from their parents—love, attention, material possessions. As they get older, everything tends to remind them of what they didn't get. At some point they start to have a look of perpetual disappointment.

If you can recognize the type early enough, it's better to avoid them, as they will inevitably make you feel guilty for something.

The Drama Magnet: They will draw you in with their exciting presence. As children, they learned that the only way to get love and attention that lasted was to enmesh their parents in their troubles and problems, which had to be large enough to engage the parents emotionally over time. As you get to know them better, you hear more stories of bickering and battles in their life, but they manage to always position themselves as the victim.

You must realize that their greatest need is to get their hooks into you by any means possible. Examine their past for evidence of the pattern and run for the hills if you suspect you are dealing with such a type.

The Big Talker: You are impressed by their ideas, the projects that they are thinking about. They need help, they need backers, and you are sympathetic, but step back for a moment and examine their record for signs of past achievements or anything tangible. You might be dealing with a type that is not overtly dangerous but can prove maddening and waste your valuable time. They themselves never finish anything. In the end, they tend to blame others for not realizing their visions—society, nebulous antagonistic forces, or bad luck.

Often such people had parents who were inconsistent, would turn on them suddenly for the smallest misdeed. Consequently their goal in life is to avoid situations in which they might open themselves up to criticism and judgment. Look carefully at their past for signs of this, and if they seem the type, be amused by their stories but take it no further.

The Sexualizer: They seem charged with sexual energy, in a way that is refreshingly unrepressed. But in truth it is compulsive and comes from a dark place. In their earliest years such people probably suffered sexual abuse in some way.

A pattern is deeply set from within and cannot be controlled—they will tend to see every relationship as potentially sexual. You cannot help or save them from their compulsion, only save yourself from entanglement with them on any level.

The Pampered Prince/Princess: They will draw you in with their regal air. Slowly you might find yourself doing favors for them, working extra hard for no pay, and not really understanding how or why. In childhood, their parents indulged them in their slightest whim and protected them from any kind of harsh intrusion from the outside world. You will notice often that when they don't get what they want, they display baby-like behavior, pouting, or even tantrums.

This is certainly the pattern for all of their intimate relationships, and unless you have a deep need to pamper others, you will find the relationship maddening, always on their terms. If you feel guilty for not helping them, it means you are hooked and should look to take care of yourself instead.

The Pleaser: You have never met anyone so nice and considerate. Then slowly you begin to have some doubts, but nothing you can put your finger on. These types are consummate courtiers, and they have developed their niceness not out of a genuine affection for their fellow humans but as a defense mechanism. Perhaps they had harsh and punishing parents who scrutinized their every action.

Just as when they were children, behind the smiles and flattery is a great deal of resentment at the role they have to play. You must be on your guard with people who actively exert so much charm and politeness, past the point of what is natural.

The Savior: You cannot believe your good luck—you have met someone who will save you from your difficulties and troubles. In the beginning it is all quite seductive, but your doubts begin the moment you want to assert your independence and do things on your own.

In childhood, these types often had to become the caregivers of their own mother, father, or siblings. This sets a pattern: they gain their greatest satisfaction from rescuing people, from being the caregiver and savior. But you can detect the compulsive aspect of this behavior by their need to control you. If they are willing to let you stand on your own two feet after some initial help, then they are truly noble. If not, it is really about the power they can exercise. In any event, it is always best to cultivate self-reliance and tell saviors to save themselves.

The Easy Moralizer: They communicate a sense of outrage at this bit of injustice or that, and they are quite eloquent. But sometimes you detect cracks in their righteous veneer. They don't treat their employees so well; they are condescending to their spouse; they may have a secret life or vice you catch glimpses of. As children, they were often made to feel guilty for their own strong impulses and desires for pleasure. They were punished and tried to repress these impulses.

In truth they are secretly drawn toward what they condemn, which is why they will inevitably have a secret side. Notice their lack of empathy early on and keep your distance.

The Superior Character

This law is simple and inexorable: you have a set character. It was formed out of elements that predate your conscious awareness. From deep within you, this character compels you to repeat actions, strategies, and decisions. The brain is structured to facilitate this: once you think and take a particular action, a neural pathway is formed that leads you to do it again and again. And in relation to this law, you can go in one of two directions, each one determining more or less the course of your life.

The first direction is ignorance and denial. You don't take notice of the patterns in your life; you don't accept the idea that your earliest years left a deep and lasting imprint that compels you to behave in certain ways. You imagine that your character is completely plastic, and that you can re-create yourself at will. You can follow the same path to power and fame as someone else, even though they come from very different circumstances. The concept of a set character can seem like a prison, and many people secretly want to be taken outside themselves, through drugs, alcohol, or video games. The result of such denial is simple: the compulsive behavior and the patterns become even more set into place. You cannot move against the grain of your character or wish it away. It is too powerful.

The other direction is harder to take, but it is the only path that leads to true power and the formation of a superior character. It works in the following manner: You examine yourself as thoroughly as possible. You look at the deepest layers of your character. You look at your primal inclinations—those subjects and activities you are naturally drawn to. You examine the quality of attachments you formed with your parents, looking at your current relationships as the best sign of this. You look with rigorous honesty at your own mistakes and the patterns that continually hold you back. You know your limitations—those situations in which you do not do your best. You also become aware of the natural strengths in your character that have survived past adolescence.

Now, with this awareness, you are no longer the captive of your character, compelled to endlessly repeat the same strategies and mistakes. As you see yourself falling into one of your usual patterns, you can catch yourself in time and step back. You may not be able to completely eliminate such patterns, but with practice you can mitigate their effects. Knowing your limitations, you will not try your hand at things for which you have no capacity or inclination. Instead, you will choose career paths that suit you and mesh with your character. In general, you accept and embrace your character. Your desire is not to become someone else but to be more thoroughly yourself, realizing your true potential. You can see your character as the clay that you will work with, slowly transforming your very weaknesses into strengths. You do not run away from your flaws but rather see them as a true source of power.

This is the alchemy that you must use on yourself. If you are a hyperperfectionist who likes to control everything, you must redirect this energy into some productive work instead of using it on people. Your attention to detail and high standards are a positive, if you channel them correctly. If you are a pleaser, you have developed courtier skills and real charm. If you can see the source of this trait, you can control the compulsive and defensive aspect of it and use it as a genuine social skill that can bring you great power. If you are highly sensitive and prone to take things personally, you can work to redirect this into active empathy, and transform this flaw into an asset to use for positive social purposes. If you have a rebellious character, you have a natural dislike of conventions and the usual ways of doing things. Channel this into some kind of innovative work, instead of compulsively insulting and alienating people. For each weakness there is a corresponding strength.

Finally, you need to also refine or cultivate those traits that go into a strong character—resilience under pressure, attention to detail, the ability to complete things, to work with a team, to be tolerant of people's differences. The only way to do so is to work on your habits, which go into the slow formation of your character. For instance, you train yourself to not react in the moment by repeatedly placing yourself in stressful or adverse situations in order to get used to them. In boring everyday tasks you cultivate greater patience and attention to detail. You deliberately take on tasks slightly above your level. In completing them, you have to work harder, helping you establish more discipline and better work habits. You train yourself to continually think of what is best for the team. You also search out others who display a strong character and associate with them as much as possible. In this way you can assimilate their energy and their habits. And to develop some flexibility in your own character, always a sign of strength, you occasionally shake yourself up, trying out some new strategy or way of thinking, doing the opposite of what you would normally do.

With such work you will no longer be a slave to the character created by your earliest years and the compulsive behavior it leads to. Even further, you can now actively shape your very character and the fate that goes with it.

> In anything, it is a mistake to think one can
> perform an action or behave in a certain way once
> and no more. (The mistake of those who say: "Let
> us slave away and save every penny till we are
> thirty, then we will enjoy ourselves." At thirty they

will have a bent for avarice and hard work, and will never enjoy themselves any more ...) What one does, one will do again, indeed has probably already done in the distant past. The agonizing thing in life is that it is our own decisions that throw us into this rut, under the wheels that crush us. (The truth is that, even before making those decisions, we were going in that direction.) A decision, an action, are infallible omens of what we shall do another time, not for any vague, mystic, astrological reason but because they result from an automatic reaction that will repeat itself.

—Cesare Pavese

5

Become an Elusive Object of Desire

——— ✧ ———

The Law of Covetousness

Absence and presence have very primal effects upon us. Too much presence suffocates; a degree of absence spurs our interest. We are marked by the continual desire to possess what we do not have—the object projected by our fantasies. Learn to create some mystery around you, to use strategic absence to make people desire your return, to want to possess you. Dangle in front of others what they are missing most in life, what they are forbidden to have, and they will go crazy with desire. The grass is always greener on the other side of the fence. Overcome this weakness in yourself by embracing your circumstance, your fate.

At last I have what I wanted. Am I happy? Not really. But what's missing? My soul no longer has that piquant activity conferred by desire ... Oh, we shouldn't delude ourselves—pleasure isn't in the fulfillment, but in the pursuit.

—*Pierre-Augustin Caron de Beaumarchais*

Keys to Human Nature

By nature, we humans are not easily contented with our circumstances. By some perverse force within us, the moment we possess something or get what we want, our minds begin to drift toward something new and different, to imagine we can have better. The more distant and unattainable this new object, the greater is our desire to have it. We can call this the *grass-is-always-greener syndrome*, the psychological equivalent of an optical illusion—if we get too close to the grass, to that new object, we see that is not really so green after all.

Such a syndrome can be explained by three qualities of the human brain. The first is known as *induction,* how something positive generates a contrasting negative image in our mind. What this means is that whenever we see or imagine something, our minds cannot help but see or imagine the opposite. If we are forbidden by our culture to think a particular thought or entertain a particular desire, that taboo instantly brings to mind the very thing we are forbidden. Every no sparks a corresponding yes. We cannot control this vacillation in the mind between contrasts. This predisposes us to think about and then desire exactly what we do not have.

Second, complacency would be a dangerous evolutionary trait for a conscious animal such as humans. If our early ancestors had been prone to feeling content with present circumstances, they would not have been sensitive enough to possible dangers that lurked in the most apparently safe environments. We no longer live in savannas or forests teeming with life-threatening predators and natural dangers, but our brains are wired as if we were. We are inclined therefore toward a continual negative bias, which often consciously is expressed through complaining and griping.

Finally, what is real and what is imagined are both experienced similarly in the brain. This has been demonstrated through various experiments in which subjects who imagine something produce electrical and chemical activity in their brains that is remarkably similar to when they actually live out what they are imagining, all of this shown through functional magnetic resonance imaging (fMRI). Reality can be quite harsh and is full of limits and problems. But in our imagination we can voyage beyond these limits and entertain all kinds of possibilities. Our imagination is essentially limitless. And what we imagine has almost the force of what we actually experience. And so we become creatures who are continually prone to imagining something better than present circumstances and feeling some pleasure in the release from reality that our imagination brings us.

All of this makes the grass-is-always-greener syndrome inevitable in our psychological makeup. We should not moralize or complain about this possible flaw in human nature. It is a part of the mental life of each one of us, and it has many benefits. It is the source of our ability to think of new possibilities and innovate. It is what has made our imagination such a powerful instrument. And on the flip side it is the material out of which we can move, excite, and seduce people.

Knowing how to work on people's natural covetousness is a timeless art that we depend on for all forms of persuasion. The problem we face today is not that people have suddenly stopped coveting but quite the opposite: that we are losing our connection to this art and the power that goes with it.

We see evidence of this in personal relationships. More and more people have come to believe that others should simply desire them for who they are. This means revealing as much as they can about themselves, exposing all of their likes and dislikes, and making themselves as familiar as possible. They leave no room for imagination or fantasy, and when the man or woman they want loses interest in them, they go online to rant at the superficiality of men or the fecklessness of women.

People may point to all of this as evidence that we humans are becoming more honest and truthful, but human nature does not change within a few generations. People have become more obvious and forthright not out of some deep moral calling but out of increasing self-absorption and overall laziness. It requires no effort to simply be oneself or to blast one's message. And the lack of effort simply results in a lack of effect on other people's psychology. It means that people's interest in you will be paper thin. Their attention will quickly move on and you will not see the reason for this. Do not swallow the easy moralism of the day, which urges honesty at the expense of desirability. Go in the opposite direction. With so few people out there who understand the art of desirability, it affords you endless opportunities to shine and exploit people's repressed fantasies.

Strategies for Stimulating Desire

The key to making this law work for you is to objectify yourself and what you produce. Once made public, your work is an object completely divorced from your own hopes and dreams, and it inspires emotions that are weak and strong. To the degree that you can see yourself and what you produce as objects that people perceive in their own manner, you have the power to alter their perceptions and create objects of desire.

The following are the three main strategies for creating such objects.

Know how and when to withdraw. This is the essence of the art. You have a presence that people see and interpret. If you are too obvious with this, if people can read you too easily and figure you out, if you show your needs too visibly, then they will unconsciously begin to have a degree of disrespect; over time they will lose interest. Your presence must have a touch of coldness to it, as if you feel like you could do without others. This signals to people that you consider yourself worthy of respect, which unconsciously heightens your value in their eyes. It makes people want to chase after you. This touch of coldness is the first form of withdrawal that you must practice. Add to this a bit of blankness and ambiguity as to who you are. Your opinions, values, and tastes are never too obvious to people. This gives them room to read into you what they want. What you want in general is to create an air of mystery and to attract interpretations.

Once you sense that you have engaged people's imagination, that you have your hooks in them, then you must use physical absence and withdrawal. You are not so available. A day or week can go by without your presence. You create a feeling of emptiness inside them, a touch of pain. You occupy increasing amounts of their mental space in these absences. They come to want more of you, not less.

With the work you produce you can create similar covetous effects. Always leave the presentation and the message relatively open-ended. People can read into your work several interpretations. Never define exactly how they should take or use it.

Keep in mind the following: the more active our imagination becomes, the greater the pleasure we derive from it. When we view an abstract painting that evokes dreams or fantasies, or see a film that is not easily interpreted, or hear a joke or advertisement that is ambiguous, *we* are the ones who do the interpreting, and we find it exciting to be able to exercise our imagination in this way. Through your work you want to stimulate this pleasure for people to the maximum degree.

Create rivalries of desire. Human desire is never an individual phenomenon. We are social creatures and what we want almost always reflects what other people want. This stems from our earliest years. We saw the attention that our parents could give us (the object we first coveted) as a zero-sum game. If our siblings receive a lot of attention, then there would be less for us. We had to compete with them and with others to get attention and affection. When we saw our siblings or friends receive something—a gift or a favor—it sparked a competitive desire to have the same thing. If some object or person was not desired by others, we tended to see it as something indifferent or distasteful—there must be something wrong with it.

This becomes a lifelong pattern. For some it is more overt. In relationships they are interested only in men or women who are already taken, who are clearly desired by a third party. Their desire is to take away this loved object, to triumph over the other person, a dynamic that most certainly has roots in their childhood. If other people are making money through some new gimmick, they want not only to participate but to corner the market. For others it is subtler. They see people possessing something that seems exciting, and their desire is not to take but to share and participate in the experience. In either direction, when we see people or things desired by others, it drives up the value.

You must learn how to exploit this. If you can somehow create the impression that others desire you or your work, you will pull people into your current without having to say a word or impose yourself. They will come to you. You must strive to surround yourself with this social aura, or at least create the illusion.

You can create this effect in several ways. You manage it so that your object is seen or heard everywhere, even encouraging piracy if necessary. You don't directly intervene. This will inevitably spark some kind of viral pull. You can speed up this process by feeding rumors or stories about the object through various media. People will begin to talk and the word of mouth will spread the effect. Even negative comments or controversy will do the trick, sometimes even better than praise. It will give your objects a provocative and transgressive edge. Anyway, people are drawn toward the negative. Your silence or lack of overt direction of the message will allow people to run wild with their own stories and interpretations. You can also get important people or tastemakers to talk about it and fan the flames. What you are offering, they say, is new, revolutionary, something not seen or heard of before. You are trafficking in the future, in trends. At a certain point, enough people will feel the pull and will not want to be left out, which will pull in others. The only problem in this game is that in the world today you have much competition for these viral effects and the public is incredibly fickle. You must be a master not only at setting off these chain reactions but at renewing them or creating new ones.

As an individual you must make it clear that people desire you, that you have a past—not too much of a past to inspire mistrust but enough to signal that others have found you desirable. You want to be indirect in this. You want them to hear stories of your past. You want them to literally see the attention you receive from men or women, all of this without your saying a word. Any bragging or explicit signaling of this will neutralize the effect.

In any negotiating situation you must always strive to bring in a third or fourth party to vie for your services, creating a rivalry of desire. This will immediately enhance your value, not just in terms of a bidding war but also in the fact that people will see that others covet you.

Use induction. We may think that we live in a time of great freedom compared with the past, but in fact we live in a world that is more regulated than ever before. Our every move is followed digitally. There are more laws than ever governing all aspects of human behavior. Political correctness, which has always existed, can be more intense because of how visible we have become on social media. Secretly most of us feel bothered or crushed by all of these constraints on our physical and mental movement. We yearn for what is transgressive and beyond the limits that are set for us. We can easily be pulled toward that repressed no or yes.

You want to associate your object with something ever so slightly illicit, unconventional, or politically advanced. One illicit desire that almost all people share is voyeurism. To peek inside the private lives of others violates strict social taboos on privacy, and yet everyone feels the pull to see what is going on behind people's doors. You can incorporate voyeurism into your work by giving the impression you are revealing secrets that should really not be shared. Some will be outraged but everyone will be curious. These could be secrets about yourself and how you accomplished what you did, or it could be about others, what happens behind the closed doors of powerful people and the laws that they operate by.

In any event, what you offer should be new, unfamiliar, and exotic, or at least presented as such. The contrast to what is out there, so numbingly conventional, will create a covetous pull.

Finally, dangle in front of people the prospect of grasping the unattainable or the impossible. Life is full of all kinds of irritating limits and difficulties. To become wealthy or successful requires great effort. We are locked inside our own character and cannot become someone else. We cannot recover our lost youth or the health that went with it. Every day brings us closer to death, the ultimate limit. Your object, however, offers the fantasy of a quick path to wealth and success, of recovering lost youth, of becoming a new person, and even of conquering death itself. People will grasp greedily at such things because they are considered so impossible. By the law of induction we can imagine all of these shortcuts and fantasies (just as we can imagine a unicorn), which gives us the desire to reach them, and imagining them is almost like experiencing them.

Remember: it is not possession but desire that secretly impels people. To possess something inevitably brings about some disappointment and sparks the desire for something new to pursue. You are preying upon the human need for fantasies and the pleasures of chasing after them. In this sense your efforts must be continually renewed. Once people get what they want or possess you, your value and their respect for you immediately begin to lower. Keep withdrawing, surprising, and stimulating the chase. As long as you do, you have the power.

The Supreme Desire

Our path must always be toward greater awareness of our nature. We must see within ourselves the grass-is-always-greener syndrome at work and how it continually impels us to certain actions. We need to be able to distinguish between what is positive and productive in our covetous tendencies and what is negative and counterproductive. On the positive side, feeling restless and discontented can motivate us to search for something better and to not settle for what we have. It enlarges our imagination as we consider other possibilities instead of the circumstances we face. As we get older, we tend to become more complacent, and renewing the restlessness of our earlier years can keep us youthful and our minds active.

This restlessness, however, must be under conscious control. Often our discontent is merely chronic; our desire for change is vague and a reflection of our boredom. This leads to a waste of precious time. We are unhappy with the way our career is going and so we make a big change, which requires learning new skills and acquiring new contacts. We enjoy the newness of it all. But several years later we again feel the stirring of discontent. This new path isn't right either. We would have been better off thinking about this more deeply, homing in on those aspects of our previous career that did not click and trying for a more gentle change, choosing a line of work related to the previous one but requiring an adaptation of our skills.

With relationships, we can spend our life searching for the perfect man or woman and end up largely alone. There is nobody perfect. Instead, it is better to come to terms with the flaws of the other person and accept them or even find some charm in their weaknesses. Calming down our covetous desires, we can then learn the arts of compromise and how to make a relationship work, which never come easily or naturally.

Instead of constantly chasing after the latest trends and modeling our desires on what others find exciting, we should spend our time getting to know our own tastes and desires better, so that we can distinguish what is something we truly need or want from that which has been manufactured by advertising or viral effects.

Life is short and we have only so much energy. Led by our covetous desires, we can waste so much time in futile searches and changes. In general, do not constantly wait and hope for something better, but rather make the most of what you have.

Consider it this way: You are embedded in an environment that consists of the people you know and the places you frequent. This is your reality. Your mind is being continually drawn far away from this reality, because of human nature. You dream of traveling to exotic places, but if you go there, you merely drag with you your own discontent frame of mind. You search for entertainment that will bring you new fantasies to feed upon. You read books filled with ideas that have no relation to your daily life, that are full of empty speculations about things that only half exist. And none of this turmoil and ceaseless desire for what is most distant ever leads to anything fulfilling—it only stirs up more chimeras to pursue. In the end you cannot escape from yourself.

On the other hand, reality beckons you. To absorb your mind in what is nearest, instead of most distant, brings a much different feeling. With the people in your circle, you can always connect on a deeper level. There is much you will never know about the people you deal with, and this can be a source of endless fascination. You can connect more deeply to your environment. The place where you live has a deep history that you can immerse yourself in. Knowing your environment better will present many opportunities for power. As for yourself, you have mysterious corners you can never fully understand. In trying to know yourself better, you can take charge of your own nature instead of being a slave to it. And your work has endless possibilities for improvement and innovation, endless challenges for the imagination. These are the things that are closest to you and compose your real, not virtual world.

In the end what you really must covet is a deeper relationship to reality, which will bring you calmness, focus, and practical powers to alter what it is possible to alter.

> It is advisable to let everyone of your acquaintance—whether man or woman—feel now and then that you could very well dispense with their company. This will consolidate friendship. Nay, with most people there will be no harm in occasionally mixing a grain of disdain with your treatment of them; that will make them value your friendship all the more ... But if we really think very highly of a person, we should conceal it from him like a crime. This is not a very gratifying thing to do, but it is right. Why, a dog will not bear being treated too kindly, let alone a man!
>
> —*Arthur Schopenhauer*

6

Elevate Your Perspective

—— ✧ ——

The Law of Shortsightedness

It is in the animal part of your nature to be most impressed by what you can see and hear in the present—the latest news reports and trends, the opinions and actions of the people around you, whatever seems the most dramatic. This is what makes you fall for alluring schemes that promise quick results and easy money. This is also what makes you overreact to present circumstances—becoming overly exhilarated or panicky as events turn one direction or the other. Learn to measure people by the narrowness or breadth of their vision; avoid entangling yourself with those who cannot see the consequences of their actions, who are in a continual reactive mode. They will infect you with this energy. Your eyes must be on the larger trends that govern events, on that which is not immediately visible. Never lose sight of your long-term goals. With an elevated perspective, you will have the patience and clarity to reach almost any objective.

I can calculate the motion of heavenly bodies, but
not the madness of people.

—*Sir Isaac Newton*

Keys to Human Nature

In the present moment we lack perspective. With the passage of time, we gain more information and see more of the truth; what was invisible to us in the present now becomes visible in retrospect. Time is the greatest teacher of them all, the revealer of reality.

We can compare this to the following visual phenomenon: At the base of a mountain, in a thick forest, we have no ability to get our bearings or to map out our surroundings. We see only what is before our eyes. If we begin to move up the side of the mountain, we can see more of our surroundings and how they relate to other parts of the landscape. The higher we go, the more we realize that what we thought further below was not quite accurate, was based on a slightly distorted perspective. At the top of the mountain we have a clear panoramic view of the scene and perfect clarity as to the lay of the land.

For us humans, locked in the present moment, it is as if we are living at the base of the mountain. What is most apparent to our eyes—the other people around us, the surrounding forest—gives us a limited, skewed vision of reality. The passage of time is like a slow ascent up the mountain. The emotions we felt in the present are no longer so strong; we can detach ourselves and see things more clearly. The further we ascend with the passage of time, the more information we add to the picture. What we saw three months after the fact is not quite as accurate as what we come to know a year later.

It would seem, then, that wisdom tends to come to us when it is too late, mostly in hindsight. But there is in fact a way for us humans to manufacture the effect of time, to give ourselves an expanded view in the present moment. We can call this the *farsighted perspective*, and it requires the following process.

First, facing a problem, conflict, or some exciting opportunity, we train ourselves to detach from the heat of the moment. We work to calm down our excitement or our fear. We get some distance.

Next we start to deepen and widen our perspective. In considering the nature of the problem we are confronting, we don't just grab for an immediate explanation, but instead we dig deeper and consider other possibilities, other possible motivations for the people involved. We force ourselves to look at the overall context of the event, not just what immediately grabs our attention. We imagine as best we can the negative consequences of the various strategies we are contemplating. We consider how the problem or the apparent opportunity might play itself out over time, how other problems or issues not apparent in the moment might suddenly loom larger than what we are immediately dealing with. We focus on our long-term goals and realign our priorities in the present according to them.

In other words, this process involves *distance* from the present, a *deeper* look at the source of the problems, a *wider* perspective on the overall context of the situation, and a look *further* into the future—including the consequences of our actions and our own long-term priorities.

As we go through this process, certain options and explanations will begin to seem more logical and realistic than others that grabbed us in the moment. We add to this the lessons we have learned over the years about our own patterns of behavior. In this way, though we cannot re-create the full effect that time has on our thinking, we can approximate it. Most often the passing months give us even more information and reveal better options for us to have taken. We are manufacturing this effect in the present by widening what we consider and opening our minds. We are moving up the mountain. Such an elevated perspective can calm us down and make it easier for us to maintain our presence of mind as events unfold.

If possible, avoid deep contact with those whose time frame is narrow, who are in continual react mode, and strive to associate with those with an expanded awareness of time.

Four Signs of Shortsightedness and Strategies to Overcome Them

Most of us imagine that we engage in some form of long-term thinking: after all, we have goals and plans. But really we are fooling ourselves. Most of the time we are improvising and reacting to events with insufficient information. Basically we are in denial about this because it is hard to have perspective about our own decision-making process.

The best way to overcome this is to recognize the clear signs of shortsighted thinking in our own lives. As with most elements of human nature, awareness is the key. Only by seeing these signs can we combat them. The following are the four most common manifestations of short-term thinking:

1. Unintended consequences. Alarmed by something in the present, we grab for a solution without thinking deeply about the context, the roots of the problem, the possible unintended consequences that might ensue. Because we mostly react instead of think, our actions are based on insufficient information.

Invariably in these cases people's thinking is remarkably simple and lazy: action A leads to result B. A variation on this, one that is quite common in the modern world, is to believe that if people have good intentions, good things should be the result. If a politician is honest and means well, he or she will bring about the desired results. In fact, people with the noblest intentions are often blinded by feelings of self-righteousness and do not consider the complex and often malevolent motivations of others.

Nonconsequential thinking is a veritable plague in the world today that is only growing worse with the speed and ease of access to information, which gives people the illusion that they are informed and have thought deeply about things. Related to this is a gradual disconnect from history itself, as people tend to view present events as if they were isolated in time.

Any phenomenon in the world is by nature complex. The people you deal with are equally complex. Any action sets off a limitless chain of reactions. It is never so simple as A leads to B. B will lead to C, to D, and beyond. Other actors will be pulled into the drama and it is hard to predict their motivations and responses. You cannot possibly map out these chains or get a complete handle on consequences. But by making your thinking more consequential you can at least become aware of the more obvious negative consequences that could ensue, and this often spells the difference between success and disaster. You want depth of thinking, to go to several degrees in imagining the permutations, as far as your mind can go.

Often, going through this process will convince you of the wisdom of doing nothing, of waiting.

While this mode of thinking is important for individuals, it can be even more crucial for large organizations, where there is a lot at stake for many people. In any group or team, put at least one person in charge of gaming out all of the possible consequences of a strategy or line of action, preferably someone with a skeptical and prudent frame of mind. You can never go too far in this process, and the time and money spent will be well rewarded as you avoid potential catastrophes and develop more solid plans.

2. Tactical hell. You find yourself embroiled in several struggles or battles. You seem to get nowhere but you feel like you have invested so much time and energy already that it would be a tremendous waste to give up. You have actually lost sight of your long-term goals, what you're really fighting for. Instead it has become a question of asserting your ego and proving you are right. Often we see this dynamic in marital spats: it is no longer about repairing the relationship but about imposing one's point of view. At times, caught in these battles, you feel defensive and petty, your spirit drawn downward. This is almost a sure sign that you have descended into tactical hell. Our minds are designed for strategic thinking—calculating several moves in advance toward our goals. In tactical hell you can never raise your perspective high enough to think in that manner. You are constantly reacting to the moves of this or that person, embroiled in their dramas and emotions, going around in circles.

The only solution is to back out temporarily or permanently from these battles, particularly if they are occurring on several fronts. You need some detachment and perspective. Get your ego to calm down. Remind yourself that winning an argument or proving your point really gets you nowhere in the long run. Win through your actions, not your words. Start to think again about your long-term goals. Create a ladder of values and priorities in your life, reminding yourself of what really matters to you. If you determine that a particular battle is in fact important, with a greater sense of detachment you can now plot a more strategic response.

More often than not you will realize that certain battles are not worth it in the end. They are a waste of valuable energy and time, which should be high on your scale of values. It is always better to walk away from a circular battle, no matter how deeply you feel personally invested in it. Your energy and your spirit are important considerations. Feeling petty and frustrated can have reverberating consequences for your ability to think strategically and reach your goals. Going through the process delineated above in the Keys will naturally elevate your perspective and put your mind on the strategic plane. And in life as in warfare, strategists will always prevail over tacticians.

3. Ticker tape fever. During the run-up to the 1929 crash on Wall Street, many people had become addicted to playing the stock market, and this addiction had a physical component—the sound of the ticker tape that electronically registered each change in a stock's price. Hearing that clicking noise indicated something was happening, somebody was trading and making a fortune. Many felt drawn to the sound itself, which felt like the heartbeat of Wall Street. We no longer have the ticker tape. Instead many of us have become addicted to the minute-by-minute news cycle, to "what's trending," to the Twitter feed, which is often accompanied by a ping that has its own narcotic effects. We feel like we are connected to the very flow of life itself, to events as they change in real time, and to other people who are following the same instant reports.

This need to know instantly has a built-in momentum. Once we expect to have some bit of news quickly, we can never go back to the slower pace of just a year ago. In fact, we feel the need for more information more quickly. Such impatience tends to spill over into other aspects of life—driving, reading a book, following a film. Our attention span decreases, as well as our tolerance for any obstacles in our path.

We can all recognize signs of this nervous impatience in our own lives, but what we don't recognize is the distorting effect it has on our thinking. The trends of the moment—in business or politics—are embedded in larger trends that play out over the course of weeks and months. Such larger spans of time tend to reveal the relative weaknesses and strengths of an investment, a strategic idea, a sports team, or a political candidate, which are often the opposite of what we see in the microtrends of the moment. In isolation, a poll or stock price do not tell us much about these strengths and weaknesses. They give us the deceptive impression that what is revealed in the present will only become more pronounced with time. It is normal to want to keep up with the latest news, but to base any kind of decision on these snapshots of the moment is to run the risk of misreading the larger picture.

Furthermore, people tend to react and overreact to any negative or positive change in the present, and it becomes doubly hard to resist getting caught up in their panic or exuberance.

Here is the antidote to the fever. First and foremost we must develop patience, which is like a muscle that requires training and repetition to make it strong.

We must make an effort to slow things down and step back, wait a day or two before taking action. Second, when faced with issues that are important, we must have a clear sense of our longterm goals and how to attain them. Part of this involves assessing the relative strengths and weaknesses of the parties involved. Such clarity will allow us to withstand the constant emotional overreactions of those around us. Finally, it is important to have faith that time will eventually prove us right and to maintain our resolve.

4. Lost in trivia. You feel overwhelmed by the complexity of your work. You feel the need to be on top of all the details and global trends so you can control things better, but you are drowning in information. It is hard to see the proverbial forest for the trees. This is a sure sign that you have lost a sense of your priorities—which facts are more important, what problems or details require more attention.

You tend to take in information without considering your priorities, what really matters in the end. But the brain has its limits. Assimilating too much information leads to mental fatigue, confusion, and feelings of help-lessness. Everything begins to seem equally important. What you need is a mental filtering system based on a scale of priorities and your long-term goals. Knowing what you want to accomplish in the end will help you weed out the essential from the nonessential. You do not have to know all the details. Sometimes you need to delegate—let your subordinates handle the information gathering. Remember that greater control over events will come from realistic assessments of the situation, precisely what is made most difficult by a brain submerged in trivia.

The Farsighted Human

Most of us live within a relatively narrow time frame. We generally associate the passage of time with something negative—aging and moving closer to death. Instinctively we recoil from thinking too deeply about the future and the past, for this reminds us of the passage of time. In relation to the future we may try to think about our plans a year or two from now, but our thinking is more like a daydream, a wish, than deep analysis. In relation to the past we may have a few fond or painful memories from childhood and later years, but in general the past baffles us. We change so much with each passing year that who we were five, ten, twenty years ago might seem like a stranger to us. We don't really have a cohesive sense of who we are, a feeling of connection between the five-year-old and thirty-five-year-old versions of ourselves.

Not wanting to go too far in either direction, we mostly live within the present. We react to what we see and hear and to what others are reacting to. We live for immediate pleasures to distract us from the passage of time and make us feel more alive. But we pay a price for all this. Repressing the thought of death and aging creates a continual underlying anxiety. We are not coming to terms with reality. Continually reacting to events in the present puts us on a roller coaster ride—up and down we go with each change in fortune. This can only add to our anxiety, as life seems to pass so quickly in the immediate rush of events.

Your task as a student of human nature, and someone aspiring to reach the greater potential of the human animal, is to widen your relationship to time as much as possible, and slow it down. This means you do not see the passage of time as an enemy but rather as a great ally. Each stage in life has its advantages—those of youth are most obvious, but with age comes greater perspective. Aging does not frighten you. Death is equally your friend. It motivates you to make the most of each moment; it gives you a sense of urgency. Time is your great teacher and master. This affects you deeply in the present. Awareness that a year from now this current problem you are experiencing will hardly seem so important will help you lower your anxiety and adjust your priorities. Knowing that time will reveal the weaknesses of your plans, you become more careful and deliberative with them.

In relation to the future, you think deeply about your long-term goals. They are not vague dreams but concrete objectives, and you have mapped out a path to reach them. In relation to the past, you feel a deep sense of connection to your childhood. Yes, you are constantly changing, but these changes are on the surface and create the illusion of real change. In fact, your character was set in your earliest years, along with your inclinations toward certain activities, your likes and dislikes. As you get older, this character only becomes more apparent. Feeling organically connected to who you were in the past gives you a strong sense of identity. You know what you like and dislike, you know who you are. This will help you maintain your self-love, which is so critical in resisting the descent into deep narcissism and in helping you to develop empathy. Also, you will pay greater attention to the mistakes and lessons of the past, which those who are locked in the present tend to repress.

Like everyone, you enjoy the present and its passing pleasures. You are not a monk. You connect to the trends of the moment and to the current flow of life. But you derive even greater pleasure from reaching your long-term goals and overcoming adversity. This expanded relationship to time will have a definite effect on you. It will make you calmer, more realistic, more in tune with the things that matter. It will also make you a superior strategist in life, able to resist people's inevitable overreactions to what is happening in the present and to see further into the future, a potential power that we humans have only begun to tap into.

The years teach much which the days never know.
—*Ralph Waldo Emerson*

7

Soften People's Resistance by Confirming Their Self-opinion

---- ✧ ----

The Law of Defensiveness

Life is harsh and people competitive. We naturally must look after our own interests. We also want to feel that we are independent, doing our own bidding. That is why when others try to persuade or change us, we become defensive and resistant. To give in challenges our need to feel autonomous. That is why to get people to move from their defensive positions you must always make it seem like what they are doing is of their own free will. Creating a feeling of mutual warmth helps soften people's resistance and makes them want to help. Never attack people for their beliefs or make them feel insecure about their intelligence or goodness—that will only strengthen their defensiveness and make your task impossible. Make them feel that by doing what you want they are being noble and altruistic—the ultimate lure. Learn to tame your own stubborn nature and free your mind from its defensive and close position, unleashing your creative powers.

The true spirit of conversation consists more in bringing out the cleverness of others than in showing a great deal of it yourself; he who goes away pleased with himself and his own wit is also greatly pleased with you. Most men ... seek less to be instructed, and even to be amused, than to be praised and applauded.

—*Jean de La Bruyère*

Keys to Human Nature

From early on in life we humans develop a defensive and self-protective side to our personality. It begins in early childhood as we cultivate a sense of personal physical space that others should not violate. It later expands into a feeling of personal dignity—people should not coerce or manipulate us into doing things we don't want to. We should be free to choose what we desire. These are necessary developments in our growth as socialized humans.

By the time we reach our twenties, we have all developed systems of defense, but in certain circumstances our inner walls can come tumbling down. For instance, during a night of revelry with friends, perhaps after some drinking, we feel bonded with others and not judged by them. In another instance, perhaps we attend some public rally and hear an inspiring speaker advocating for a cause. Feeling on the same page as hundreds of others, caught up in the group spirit, we suddenly feel called to action and to work for the cause—something we might normally resist.

Creating this feeling of validation is the golden key that will unlock people's defenses. And we cannot survive and thrive in this highly competitive world without possessing such a power.

We must discover the power that we can possess by giving people the validation they crave and lowering their defenses. And the key to making this happen in a realistic and strategic manner is to fully understand a fundamental law of human nature.

This law is as follows: People have a perception about themselves that we shall call their *self-opinion*. This self-opinion can be accurate or not—it doesn't matter. What matters is how people perceive their own character and worthiness. And there are three qualities to people's self-opinion that are nearly universal: "I am autonomous, acting of my own free will"; "I am intelligent in my own way"; and "I am basically good and decent."

When it comes to the first universal (I am acting of my own free will), if we join a group, or believe something, or buy a product, it is because we *choose* to do so. The truth might be that we were manipulated or succumbed to peer pressure, but we will tell ourselves something else.

With the second universal (I am intelligent), we may realize we are not on the level of an Einstein, but in our field, in our own way, we are intelligent. People are generally never comfortable with the thought that they could be gullible and less than intelligent. If they have to admit they are not smart in the conventional way, they will at least think they are cleverer than others.

With the third universal (I am a good person), we like to see ourselves as supporting the right causes. We treat people well. We are a team player. If we happen to be the boss and we like to instill discipline in the troops, we call it "tough love." We are acting for the good of others.

When you try to convince people of something, one of three things will happen. First, you might inadvertently challenge a particular aspect of their self-opinion. If this happens, you make people even more defensive and resistant.

Second, you can leave their self-opinion in a neutral position—neither challenged nor confirmed. In this scenario people remain resistant and dubious, but you have at least not tightened them up, and you have some room to maneuver them with your rational arguments.

Third, you can actively confirm their self-opinion. Their minds open, making them susceptible to suggestion and insinuation. If they decide to help you, they feel like they are doing this of their own free will.

Your task is simple: instill in people a feeling of inner security. Mirror their values; show that you like and respect them. Make them feel you appreciate their wisdom and experience. Generate an atmosphere of mutual warmth. Get them to laugh along with you, instilling a feeling of rapport. All of this works best if the feelings are not completely faked. By exercising your empathy, by getting inside their perspective, you are more likely to genuinely feel at least a part of such emotions. Practice this often enough and confirming people's self-opinion will become your default position—you will have a loosening-up effect on almost everyone you encounter.

The greatest obstacle you will face in developing these powers comes from a cultural prejudice against the very idea of influence: "Why can't we all just be honest and transparent with one another, and simply ask for what we want? Why can't we just let people be who they are and not try to change them? Being strategic is ugly and manipulative." First, when people tell you such things, you should be on guard. We humans cannot stand feelings of powerlessness. We need to have influence or we become miserable. The honestymongers are no different, but because they need to believe in their angelic qualities, they cannot square this self-opinion with the need to have influence. And so they often become passive-aggressive, pouting and making others feel guilty as a means of getting what they want. Never take people who say such things at face value.

Second, we humans cannot avoid trying to influence others. Everything we say or do is examined and interpreted by others for clues as to our intentions. As social animals we cannot avoid constantly playing the game, whether we are conscious of this or not.

Since the game is unavoidable, better to be skillful at it than in denial or merely improvising in the moment. In the end, being good at influence is actually more socially beneficial than the moral stance. By having this power, we can influence people who have dangerous or antisocial ideas. Becoming proficient at persuasion requires that we immerse ourselves in the perspective of others, exercising our empathy. We might have to abide by the cultural prejudice and nod our heads in agreement about the need for complete honesty, but inwardly we must realize that this is nonsense and practice what is necessary for our own well-being.

Five Strategies for Becoming a Master Persuader

The following five strategies—distilled from the examples of the greatest influencers in history—are designed to help you focus more deeply on your targets and create the kinds of emotional effects that will help lower people's resistance. It would be wise to put all five into practice.

1. Transform yourself into a deep listener. In the normal flow of a conversation, our attention is divided. The reason for this is simple: we are more interested in our own thoughts, feelings, and experience than in those of the other person. If this were not the case, we would find it relatively easy to listen with full attention. The usual prescription is to talk less and listen more, but this is meaningless advice as long as we prefer our own internal monologue. The only solution is to somehow be *motivated* to reverse this dynamic.

Think of it this way: You know your own thoughts

only too well. But each person you encounter represents an undiscovered country full of surprises. Imagine for a moment that you could step inside people's minds and what an amazing journey that could be. People who seem quiet and dull often have the strangest inner lives for you to explore. Transforming yourself into a deep listener will not only prove more amusing as you open your mind to their mind but will also provide the most invaluable lessons about human psychology.

Once you are motivated to listen, the rest is relatively simple. You must not barrage the other person with questions that make it feel like a job interview. Instead, pay attention to their nonverbal cues. You will see their eyes light up when certain topics are mentioned—you must guide the conversation in that direction. People will become chatty without realizing it. Almost everyone likes to talk about their childhood, their family, the ins and outs of their work, or some cause that is dear to them. An occasional question or comment plays off something they have said.

You are deeply absorbed in what they say, but you must feel and appear relaxed in being so. You convey that you are listening by maintaining relatively consistent eye contact and nodding as they talk. The best way to signal how deeply you are listening is to occasionally say something that mirrors what they have said, but in your own words and filtered through your own experience. In the end, the more they talk, the more they will reveal about their insecurities and unmet desires.

2. Infect people with the proper mood. As social animals, we are extremely susceptible to the moods of other people. This gives us the power to subtly infuse into people the appropriate mood for influencing them. If you are relaxed and anticipating a pleasurable experience, this will communicate itself and have a mirror-like effect on the other person. One of the best attitudes to adapt for this purpose is one of complete indulgence. You do not judge other people; you accept them as they are.

A variation of this is to infect people with a warm feeling of rapport through laughter and shared pleasures. Many studies on nonverbal cues have demonstrated the incredible power that a simple touch of people's hands or arms can have in any interaction, making them think positive things about you without their ever being aware of the source of their good opinions. Such gentle taps establish a feeling of visceral rapport, as long as you do not maintain eye contact, which will give it too much of a sexual connotation.

Keep in mind that your expectations about people are communicated to them nonverbally. By feeling particularly excited when you're meeting someone, you will communicate this to him or her in a powerful way. If there is a person of whom you will eventually ask a favor, try imagining him or her in the best light—generous and caring—if that is possible.

3. Confirm their self-opinion. Recall the universal qualities of the self-opinions of people with a high self-opinion. Here's how to approach each one of them.

Autonomy. No attempt at influence can ever work if people feel in any way that they are being coerced or manipulated. They must *choose* to do whatever it is you want them to do, or they must at least experience it as their choice. The more deeply you can create this impression, the greater your chances of success.

Your attempts at influence must always follow this logic: how can you get others to perceive the favor you want to ask for as something they already desire? Framing it as something pleasurable, as a rare opportunity, and as something other people want to do will generally have the proper effect. Another variation on this is to appeal directly to people's competitive instincts.

Finally, when giving people gifts or rewards as a possible means of winning them over to your side, it is always best to give smaller gifts or rewards than larger ones. Large gifts make it too apparent that you are trying to buy their loyalty, which will offend people's sense of independence. Some might accept large gifts out of need, but later they will feel resentful or suspicious. Smaller gifts have a better effect—people can tell themselves they deserve such things and are not being bought or bribed. In fact, such smaller rewards, spread out over time, will bind people to you in a much greater way than anything lavish.

Intelligence. The nineteenth-century British prime minister and novelist Benjamin Disraeli conceived of a clever ploy when he wrote, "If you wish to win a man's heart, allow him to confute you." You do this by beginning to disagree with a target about a subject, even with some vehemence, and then slowly come to seeing their point of view, thereby confirming not only their intelligence but also their own powers of influence. They feel ever so slightly superior to you, which is precisely what you want. They will now be doubly vulnerable to a countermove of your own. You can create a similar effect by asking people for advice. The implication is that you respect their wisdom and experience.

Lowering people's defenses in this way on matters that are not so important will give you great latitude to move them in the direction you desire and get them to concede to your desires on more important matters.

Goodness. In our daily thoughts, we constantly comfort ourselves as to the moral nature of our actions. Just as important, we want others to see us in this light.

You must never inadvertently cast doubts on this saintly self-opinion. To make positive use of this trait in people, frame what you are asking them to do as part of a larger cause that they can participate in. Keep it subtle. If you are trying to get recruits for a job, let others spread the message about the cause. Make it appear prosocial and popular. Make people want to join the group, instead of having to plead with them. Pay great attention to the words and labels you use. It is better, for instance, to call someone a team member than an employee.

To put yourself in the inferior, one-down position, you can commit some relatively harmless faux pas, even offend people in a more pronounced way, and then ask for their forgiveness. By asking for this, you imply their moral superiority, a position people love to occupy.

Finally, if you need a favor from people, do not remind them of what you have done for them in the past, trying to stimulate feelings of gratitude. Instead, remind them of the good things they have done for you in the past. This will help confirm their self-opinion: "Yes, I am generous." And once reminded, they will want to continue to live up to this image and do yet another good deed. A similar effect can come from suddenly forgiving your enemies and forging a rapprochement. In the emotional turmoil this creates, they will feel obligated to live up to the high opinion you have now shown toward them and will be extra motivated to prove themselves worthy.

4. Ally their insecurities. Everyone has particular insecurities—about their looks, their creative powers, their masculinity, their power status, their uniqueness, their popularity, et cetera. Your task is to get a bead on these insecurities through the various conversations you draw them into.

Once you've identified them, you must first be extra careful not to trigger them. Second, the best strategy is to praise and flatter those qualities that people are most insecure about.

The key to successful flattery is to make it strategic. If I know that I am particularly awful at basketball, praising me for my basketball skills in any way will ring false. But if I am *uncertain* about my skills, if I imagine I am perhaps not really so bad, then any flattery on that score can work wonders. Look for those qualities people are uncertain about and offer reassurance.

It is always better to praise people for their effort, not their talent. Everyone likes to feel that they earned their good fortune through hard work, and that is where you must aim your praise.

With people who are your equals, you have more room to flatter. With those who are your superiors, it is best to simply agree with their opinions and validate their wisdom.

Never follow up your praise with a request for help, or whatever it is you are after. Your flattery is a setup and requires the passage of some time. Do not appear too ingratiating in the first encounter or two. Better to show even a little coldness, which will give you room to warm up. After a few days you have grown to like this person, and then a few flattering words aimed at their insecurities will begin to melt their resistance. If possible, get third parties to pass along your compliments, as if they had simply overheard them. Never be too lavish in your praise or use absolutes.

A clever way to cover your tracks is to mix in some small criticisms of the person or their work, nothing that will trigger insecurities but enough to give your praise a more realistic hue: "I loved your screenplay, although I feel act two might need a little work." Be very careful when people ask you for their opinion about their work or something related to their character or their looks. They do not want the truth; they want support and confirmation given as realistically as possible. Be happy to supply this for them.

You must seem as sincere as possible. It would be

best to choose qualities to praise that you actually admire, if at all possible. In any event, what gives people away is the nonverbal cues—praise along with stiff body language or a fake smile or eyes glancing elsewhere. Try to feel some of the good emotions you are expressing so any exaggeration will seem less obvious. Keep in mind that your target must have a relatively high self-opinion. If it is low, the flattery will not jibe with how they feel about themselves and will ring hollow, whereas for those of high self-opinion it will seem only natural.

5. Use people's resistance and stubbornness.

Some people are particularly resistant to any form of influence. They will seek advice for a particular problem or symptom, only to find dozens of reasons of why the advice given won't work for them. The best thing to do is to play a game of mental judo with them. In judo you do not counter people's moves with a thrust of your own but rather encourage their aggressive energy (resistance) in order to make them fall on their own. Here are some ways to put this into practice in everyday life.

Use their emotions: In essence, the idea is not to counter people's strong emotions but to move with them and find a way to channel them in a productive direction.

Use their language: When you use people's words back at them, it has a hypnotic effect. How can they not follow what you suggest when it is exactly the words they have used?

Use their rigidity: When people are rigid in

their opposition to something, it stems from deep fear of change and the uncertainty it could bring. They must have everything on their terms and feel in control. You play into their hands if you try with all your advice to encourage change—it gives them something to react against and justifies their rigidity. They become more stubborn. Stop fighting with such people and use the actual nature of their rigid behavior to effect a gentle change that could lead to something greater. On their own, they discover something new, and on their own they might take this further, all set up by your judo maneuver.

Keep in mind the following: people often won't do what others ask them to do, because they simply want to assert their will. If you heartily agree with their rebellion and tell them to keep on doing what they're doing, it now means that if they do so they are following your advice, which is distasteful to them. They may very well rebel again and assert their will in the opposite direction, which is what you wanted all along—the essence of reverse psychology.

The Flexible Mind—Self-Strategies

As children our minds were remarkably flexible. We could learn at a rate that far surpasses our adult capacities. We can attribute much of the source of this power to our feelings of weakness and vulnerability. Sensing our inferiority in relation to those older than us, we felt highly motivated to learn. We were also genuinely curious and hungry for new information. We were open to the influence of parents, peers, and teachers.

Just as the body tightens with age, however, so does the mind. And just as our sense of weakness and vulnerability motivated the desire to learn, so does our creeping sense of superiority slowly close us off to new ideas and influences. Some may advocate that we all become more skeptical in the modern world, but in fact a far greater danger comes from the increasing closing of the mind that afflicts us as individuals as we get older, and seems to be afflicting our culture in general.

Let us define the ideal state of the mind as one that retains the flexibility of youth along with the reasoning powers of the adult. Such a mind is open to the influence of others. And just as you use strategies to melt people's resistance, you must do the same on yourself, working to soften up your rigid mental patterns.

When it comes to the ideas and opinions you hold, see them as toys or building blocks that you are playing with. Some you will keep, others you will knock down, but your spirit remains flexible and playful.

Even in writing that is inimical to your own ideas there is often something that rings true, which represents the "soul of the thing." Opening yourself up to its influence in this way should become part of your mental habits, allowing you to better understand things, even to criticize them properly.

Finally, when it comes to your own self-opinion, try to have some ironic distance from it. Make yourself aware of its existence and how it operates within you. Come to terms with the fact that you are not as free and autonomous as you like to believe. You do conform to the opinions of the groups you belong to; you do buy products because of subliminal influence; you can be manipulated. Realize as well that you are not as good as the idealized image of your self-opinion. Like everyone else, you can be quite self-absorbed and obsessed with your own agenda. With this awareness, you will not feel the need to be validated by others. Instead you will work at making yourself truly independent and concerned with the welfare of others, as opposed to staying attached to the illusion of your self-opinion.

> There was something terribly enthralling in the exercise of influence. No other activity was like it. To project one's soul into some gracious form, and let it tarry there for a moment; to hear one's own intellectual views echoed back to one with all the added music of passion and youth; to convey one's temperament into another as though it were a subtle fluid or a strange perfume: there was a real joy in that—perhaps the most satisfying joy left to us in an age so limited and vulgar as our own, an age grossly carnal in its pleasures, and grossly common in its aims.
>
> —*Oscar Wilde,* The Picture of Dorian Gray

8

Change Your Circumstances by Changing Your Attitude

⸻ ⋄ ⸻

The Law of Self-sabotage

Each of us has a particular way of looking at the world, of interpreting events and the actions of people around us. This is our attitude, and it determines much of what happens to us in life. If our attitude is essentially fearful, we see the negative in every circumstance. We stop ourselves from taking chances. We blame others for mistakes and fail to learn from them. If we feel hostile or suspicious, we make others feel such emotions in our presence. We sabotage our career and relationships by unconsciously creating the circumstances we fear the most. The human attitude, however, is malleable. By making our attitude more positive, open, and tolerant of other people, we can spark a different dynamic—we can learn from adversity, create opportunities out of nothing, and draw people to us. We must explore the limits of our willpower and how far it can take us.

The greatest discovery of my generation is the fact

that human beings can alter their lives by altering their attitudes of mind.

—William James

Keys to Human Nature

We humans like to imagine that we have an objective knowledge of the world. We take it for granted that what we perceive on a daily basis is reality—this reality being more or less the same for everybody. But this is an illusion. No two people see or experience the world in the same way. What we perceive is our personal version of reality, one that is of our own creation. To realize this is a critical step in our understanding of human nature.

Each of us sees the world through a particular lens that colors and shapes our perceptions. Let us call this lens our *attitude*. The great Swiss psychologist Carl Jung defined this in the following way: "Attitude is a readiness of the psyche to act or react in a certain way ... To have an attitude means to be ready for something definite, even though this something is unconscious; for having an attitude is synonymous with an *a priori* orientation to a definite thing."

Although attitudes come in many varieties and blends, we can generally categorize them as negative and narrow or positive and expansive. Those with a negative attitude tend to operate from a basic position of fear toward life. They unconsciously want to limit what they see and experience to give them more control.

Those with a positive attitude have a much less fearful approach. They are open to new experiences, ideas, and emotions. If the attitude is like our lens on the world, the negative attitude narrows the aperture of this lens, and the positive variety expands it as far as possible.

Your task as a student of human nature is twofold: First, you must become aware of your own attitude and how it slants your perceptions. It is hard to observe this in your day-to-day life because it is so close to you, but there are ways to catch glimpses of it in action. You can see it in how you judge people once they are out of your presence. Are you quick to focus on their negative qualities and bad opinion, or are you more generous and forgiving when it comes to their flaws? You will see definite signs of your attitude in how you face adversity or resistance. Are you quick to forget or gloss over any mistakes on your part?

You will also catch signs of it in how people respond to you, particularly in a nonverbal way. Do you catch them being nervous or defensive in your presence?

Once you have a good feel for the makeup of your own attitude, its negative or positive bent, you have much greater power to alter it, to move it more in the positive direction.

Second, you must not only be aware of the role of your attitude but also believe in its supreme power to alter your circumstances. The mind and the body are one, and your thoughts affect your physical responses. People can recover much more quickly from illness through sheer desire and willpower. You are not born with fixed intelligence and inherent limits. See your brain as a miraculous organ designed for continual learning and improvement, well into old age. The rich neural connections in your brain, your creative power, are something you develop to the degree that you open yourself up to new experiences and ideas. View problems and failures as means to learn and toughen yourself up. You can get through anything with persistence. View the way people treat you as largely flowing from your own attitude, something you can control.

Do not be afraid to exaggerate the role of willpower. It is an exaggeration with a purpose. It leads to a positive self-fulfilling dynamic, and that is all you care about. See this shaping of your attitude as your most important creation in life, and never leave it to chance.

The Constricted (Negative) Attitude

People who feel particularly weak and vulnerable tend to adopt an attitude toward life that narrows what they experience so that they can reduce the possibility of unexpected events. The following are the five most common forms of the constricted attitude. Negative emotions have a binding power—a person who is angry is more prone to also feel suspicion, deep insecurities, resentment, et cetera. And so we often find combinations of these various negative attitudes, each one feeding and accentuating the other. Your goal is to recognize the various signs of such attitudes that exist in you in latent and weakened forms, and to root them out; to see how they operate in a stronger version in other people, better understanding their perspective on life; and to learn how to handle people with such attitudes.

The Hostile Attitude. Some children exhibit a hostile attitude at a very early age. The child looks out on a world that seems fraught with hostility, and their answer is to seek to control it by becoming the source of the hostility themselves. As they get older, they become adept at stimulating anger and frustration in others, which justifies their original attitude—"See, people are against me, I am disliked, and for no apparent reason."

In a relationship, a husband with a hostile attitude will accuse his wife of not really loving him. If she protests and becomes defensive, he will see this as a sign that she has to try hard to disguise the truth. If she is intimidated into silence, he sees that as a sign that he was right along. In her confusion, she can easily begin to feel some hostility on her part, confirming his opinion. People with this attitude have many other subtle tricks up their sleeve for provoking the hostility they secretly want to feel directed at them—withdrawing their cooperation on a project at just the wrong moment, constantly being late, doing a poor job, deliberately making an unfavorable first impression. But they never see themselves as playing any kind of role in instigating the reaction.

If you notice signs of this attitude in yourself, such self-awareness is a major step toward being able to get rid of it. You can also try a simple experiment: Approach people you are meeting for the first time, or only know peripherally, with various positive thoughts—"I like them," "They seem smart," et cetera. None of this is verbalized, but you do your best to feel such emotions. If they respond with something hostile or defensive, then perhaps the world is truly against you. More than likely you will not see anything that could be remotely construed as negative. In fact, you will see the opposite. Clearly, then, the source of any hostile response is you.

In dealing with the extremes of this type, struggle as best you can to not respond with the antagonism they expect. Maintain your neutrality. This will confound them and temporarily put a stop to the game they are playing.

The Anxious Attitude. These types anticipate all kinds of obstacles and difficulties in any situation they face. With people, they often expect some sort of criticism or even betrayal. All of this stimulates unusual amounts of anxiety before the fact. What they really fear is losing control of the situation. Their solution is to limit what can possibly happen, to narrow the world they deal with. This means limiting where they go and what they'll attempt. In a relationship, they will subtly dominate the domestic rituals and habits; they will seem brittle and demand extra careful attention. This will dissuade people from criticizing them. Everything must be on their terms. At work they will be ferocious perfectionists and micromanagers, eventually sabotaging themselves by trying to keep on top of too many things.

Once outside their comfort zone—the home or the relationship they dominate—they become unusually fretful.

Sometimes they can disguise their need for control as a form of love and concern. Another disguise, similar to such love, is to seek to please and cajole people in order to disarm any possible unpredictable and unfriendly action.

If you notice such tendencies in yourself, the best antidote is to pour your energies into work. As long as you rein in your perfectionist tendencies, you can channel your need to control into something productive. With people, try to slowly open yourself to their habits and pace of doing things, instead of the opposite. Deliberately place yourself in the circumstances you most dread, discovering that your fears are grossly exaggerated.

In dealing with those with this attitude, try to not feel infected with their anxiety and instead try to provide the soothing influence they so lacked in their earliest years.

The Avoidant Attitude. People with this attitude see the world through the lens of their insecurities, generally related to doubts about their competence and intelligence. As these people get older, their main goal in life is to avoid any kind of responsibility or challenge in which their self-esteem might be at stake and for which they can be judged. If they do not try too hard in life, they cannot fail or be criticized.

To enact this strategy they will constantly seek escape routes, consciously or unconsciously. They will find the perfect reason for leaving a job early and changing careers, or breaking off a relationship. In the middle of some high-stakes project they will suddenly develop an illness that will cause them to leave. They are prone to all kinds of psychosomatic maladies. Or they become alcoholics, addicts of some sort, always falling off the wagon at the right time but blaming this on the "disease" they have, and their bad upbringing that caused their addiction. Other strategies will include wasting time and starting too late on something, always with some built-in excuse for why that happened. They then cannot be blamed for the mediocre results.

You can easily recognize such people by their checkered careers and their short-term personal relationships. They may try to disguise the source of their problems by seeming saintly—they look down on success and people who have to prove themselves. Do not be fooled by their holier-than-thou front they present. Look at their actions, the lack of accomplishments, the great projects they never start on, always with a good cause.

If you notice traces of this attitude in yourself, a good strategy is to take on a project of even the smallest scale, taking it all the way to completion and embracing the prospect of failure. If you fail, you will have already cushioned the blow because you anticipated it, and inevitably it will not hurt as much as you had imagined. Your self-esteem will rise because you finally tried something and finished it. Once you diminish this fear, progress will be easy. You will want to try again. And if you succeed, all the better. Either way, you win.

When you find others with this attitude, be very wary of forming partnerships with them. At all costs avoid the temptation to help or rescue them from their negativity.

The Depressive Attitude. As children, these types did not feel loved or respected by their parents. For helpless children, it is too much to imagine that their parents could be wrong or flawed in their parenting. And so their defense is to often internalize the negative judgment and imagine that they are indeed unworthy of being loved, that there is something actually wrong with them. As adults they will anticipate abandonment, loss, and sadness in their experiences and see signs of potentially depressing things in the world around them. A strategy they will employ throughout their lives is to temporarily withdraw from life and from people. This will feed their depression and also make it something they can manage to some extent, as opposed to traumatic experiences imposed upon them.

These types often have a secret need to wound others, encouraging behavior such as betrayal or criticism that will feed their depression. They will also sabotage themselves if they experience any kind of success, feeling deep down that they don't deserve it. They will develop blocks in their work, or take criticism to mean they should not continue with their career. Depressive types can often attract people to them, because of their sensitive nature; they stimulate the desire to want to help them. But they will start to criticize and wound the ones who wish to help, then withdraw again. This push and pull causes confusion, but once under their spell it is hard to disengage from them without feeling guilty. They have a gift for making other people feel depressed in their presence. This gives them more fuel to feed off.

Most of us have depressive tendencies and moments. The best way to handle them is to be aware of their necessity—they are our body's and mind's way of compelling us to slow down, to lower our energies and withdraw. The best way to handle recurrent depression is to channel your energies into work, especially the arts. You are used to withdrawing and being alone; use such time to tap into your unconscious. Externalize your unusual sensitivity and your dark feelings into the work itself.

Never try to lift up depressive people by preaching to them about the wonderfulness of life. Instead, it is best to go along with their gloomy opinion of the world while subtly drawing them into positive experiences that can elevate their moods and energy without any direct appeal.

The Resentful Attitude. As children, these types never felt they got enough parental love and affection—they were always greedy for more attention. They carry this sense of dissatisfaction and disappointment with them throughout their lives. They are experts at scanning people's faces for signs of possible disrespect or disdain. They see everything in relation to themselves; if someone has more than they do, it is a sign of injustice, a personal affront. When they feel this lack of respect and recognition, they do not explode in anger. Instead, the hurt incubates inside them, the sense of injustice growing stronger as they reflect on this. They do not easily forget. At some point they will take their revenge in some shrewdly plotted act of sabotage or passive aggression.

Because they have a continual feeling of being wronged, they tend to project this on to the world, seeing oppressors everywhere. In this way, they often become the leader of those who feel disaffected and oppressed. If such types get power, they can become quite vicious and vengeful, finally able to vent their resentments on various victims. In general, they carry themselves with an air of arrogance; they are above others even if no one recognizes this. They carry their head a little too high; they frequently have a slight smirk or look of disdain. As they get older, they are prone to pick petty battles, unable to completely contain their resentments that have accumulated over time. Their bitter attitude pushes a lot of people away, and so they often end up congregating with others who have this attitude, as their form of commentary.

If you notice resentful tendencies within yourself, the best antidote is to learn to let go of hurts and disappointments in life. It is better to explode into anger in the moment, even if it's irrational, than to stew on slights that you have probably hallucinated or exaggerated. You must break out of the resentful cycle by becoming more generous toward people and human nature.

In dealing with such types, you must exercise

supreme caution. You can recognize them by their history of past battles and sudden breaks with people, as well as how easily they judge others. You might try to slowly gain their trust and lower their suspicions; but be aware that the longer you are around them, the more fuel you will give them for something to resent, and their response can be quite vicious. Better to avoid this type if possible.

The Expansive (Positive) Attitude

A negative, constricting attitude is designed to narrow down the richness of life at the cost of our creative powers, our sense of fulfilment, our social pleasures, and our vital energies. Without wasting another day under such conditions, your goal is to break out, to expand what you see and what you experience. You want to open the aperture of the lens as wide as you can. Here is your road map.

How to view the world: See yourself as an explorer. Most people prefer to cling to certain ideas and principles, many of them adopted early on in life. They are secretly afraid of what is unfamiliar and uncertain. They replace curiosity with conviction. By the time they are thirty, they act as if they know everything they need to know.

As an explorer you leave all that certainty behind you. Ideas are things to play with. You explore all forms of knowledge, from all cultures and time periods. You want to be challenged.

By opening the mind in this way, you will unleash unrealized creative powers, and you will give yourself great mental pleasure. As part of this, be open to exploring the insights that come from your own unconscious, as revealed in your dreams, in moments of tiredness, and in the repressed desires that leak out in certain moments.

How to view adversity: Our life inevitably involves obstacles, frustrations, pain, and separations. How we come to handle such moments in our early years plays a large role in the development of our overall attitude toward life. For many people, such difficult moments inspire them to restrict what they see and experience. Instead of learning from negative experiences, they want to repress them. Your goal is to move in the opposite direction, to embrace all obstacles as learning experiences, as means to getting stronger. In this way you embrace life itself.

Although adversity and pain are generally beyond your control, you have the power to determine your response and the fate that comes from that.

How to view yourself: As we get older, we tend to place limits on how far we can go in life. By accepting what we think to be the limits of our intelligence and creative powers, we create a self-fulfilling dynamic. You do not need to be so humble and self-effacing in this world. Such humility is not a virtue but is rather a value that people promote to help keep you down. Whatever you are doing now, you are in fact capable of much more, and by thinking that, you will create a very different dynamic.

How to view your energy and health: Although we are all mortal and subject to illnesses beyond our control, we must recognize the role that willpower plays in our health. We have all felt this to some degree or another. When we fall in love or feel excited by our work, suddenly we have more energy and recover quickly from any illnesses. When we are depressed or unusually stressed, we become prey to all kinds of ailments. Our attitude plays an enormous role in our health, one that science has begun to explore and will examine in more depth in the coming decades. In general, you can safely push yourself beyond what you think are your physical limits by feeling excited and challenged by a project or endeavor. People get old and prematurely age by accepting physical limits to what they can do, making it a self-fulfilling cycle. Those who age well continue to engage in physical activity, only moderately adjusted. You have wellsprings of energy and health you have yet to tap into.

How to view other people: First you must try to get rid of the natural tendency to take what people do and say as something personally directed at you, particularly if what they say or do is unpleasant. Even when they criticize you or act against your interest, more often than not it stems from some deep earlier pain they are reliving; you become the convenient target of frustrations and resentments that have been accumulating over the years. They are projecting their own negative feelings. If you can view people this way, you will find it easier to not react and get upset or become embroiled in some petty battle. If the person is truly malicious, by not becoming emotional yourself you will be in a better place to plot the proper countermove. You will save yourself from accumulating hurts and bitter feelings.

From this more neutral stance, you can then try to understand the people you deal with on a deeper level. The more you do this, the more tolerant you will tend to become toward people and toward human nature in general. Your open, generous spirit will make your social interactions much smoother, and people will be drawn to you.

> This is why the same external events or circumstances affect no two people alike; even with perfectly similar surroundings every one lives in a world of his own ... The world in which a man lives shapes itself chiefly by the way in which he looks at it, and so it proves different to different men; to one it is barren, dull, and superficial; to another rich, interesting, and full of meaning. On hearing of the interesting events which have happened in the course of a man's experience, many people will wish that similar things had happened in their lives too, completely forgetting that they should be

envious rather of the mental aptitude which lent those events the significance they possess when he describes them.

—*Arthur Schopenhauer*

9

Confront Your Dark Side

◇

The Law of Repression

People are rarely who they seem to be. Lurking beneath their polite, affable exterior is inevitably a dark, shadow side consisting of the insecurities and the aggressive, selfish impulses they repress and carefully conceal from public view. This dark side leaks out in behavior that will baffle and harm you. Learn to recognize the signs of the Shadow before they become toxic. See people's overt traits—toughness, saintliness, et cetera—as covering up the opposite quality. You must become aware of your own dark side. In being conscious of it you can control and channel the creative energies that lurk in your unconscious. By integrating the dark side into your personality, you will be a more complete human and will radiate an authenticity that will draw people to you.

This longing to commit a madness stays with us throughout our lives. Who has not, when standing with someone by an abyss or high up on a tower, had a sudden impulse to push the other over? And how is it that we hurt those we love although we know that remorse will follow? Our whole being is nothing but a fight against the dark forces within ourselves. To live is to war with trolls in heart and soul. To write is to sit in judgment on oneself.

–Henrik Ibsen

Keys to Human Nature

If we think about the people we know and see on a regular basis, we would have to agree that they are usually quite pleasant and agreeable. For the most part, they seem pleased to be in our company, are relatively upfront and confident, socially responsible, able to work with a team, take good care of themselves, and treat others well. But every now and then with these friends, acquaintances, and colleagues, we glimpse behavior that seems to contradict what we normally see.

What we glimpse in these moments is the dark side of their character, what the Swiss psychologist Carl Jung called the Shadow. The Shadow consists of all the qualities people try to deny about themselves and repress. This repression is so deep and effective that people are generally unaware of their Shadow; it operates unconsciously. When we experience those moments when people reveal the dark side, we can see something come over their face; their voice and body language is altered—almost as if another person is confronting us, the features of the upset child suddenly becoming visible. We *feel* their shadow as it stirs and emerges.

The Shadow lies buried deep within, but it becomes disturbed and active in moments of stress, or when deep wounds and insecurities are triggered. It also tends to emerge more as people get older. When we are young, everything seems exciting to us, including the various social roles we must play. But later in life we tire of the masks we have been wearing, and the leakage is greater.

Concealing this dark side requires energy; it can be draining to always present such a nice, confident front. And so the Shadow wants to release some of the inner tension and come back to life. You must become adept at recognizing such moments of release in others and interpreting them, seeing the outlines of the Shadow that now come forward. The following are some of the most notable signs of such release.

Contradictory behavior: This is the most eloquent sign of all. It consists of actions that belie the carefully constructed front that people present. For instance, a person who preaches morals is suddenly caught out in a very compromising situation. The strange contradictory behavior is a direct expression of the Shadow.

Emotional outbursts: A person suddenly loses his or her habitual self-control and sharply expresses deep resentments or says something biting and hurtful. In the aftermath of such a release, they may blame it on stress; they may say they did not mean any of it, when in fact the opposite is the case—the Shadow has spoken. Take what they said at face value.

Vehement denial: According to Freud, the only way that something unpleasant or uncomfortable in our unconscious can reach the conscious mind is through active denial. We express the very opposite of what is buried within. This could be a person fulminating against homosexuality, when in fact he or she feels the opposite. You must reinterpret the denials as positive expressions of Shadow desires.

"Accidental" behavior: People might talk of quitting some addiction, or not working so damned hard, or staying away from a self-destructive relationship. They then fall into the behavior they spoke of trying to avoid, blaming it on an uncontrollable illness or dependency. This salves their conscience for indulging their dark side; they simply can't help it. Ignore the justifications and see the Shadow operating and releasing. Also remember that when people are drunk and behave differently, often it is not the alcohol that is speaking but the Shadow.

Overidealization: This can serve as one of the most potent covers for the Shadow. Let us say we believe in some cause, such as the importance of transparency in our actions, particularly in politics. We see everything in black-and-white terms—our cause is moral, modern, and progressive; the other side, including doubters, is evil and reactionary.

By overidealizing a cause, person, or object, people can give free rein to the Shadow. That is their unconscious motivation. The bullying, the manipulations, the greed that comes out for the sake of the cause or product should be taken at face value, the overly strong conviction providing simple cover for repressed emotions to play themselves out.

Relating to this, in arguments people will use their powerful convictions as a perfect way to disguise their desires to bully and intimidate.

Projection: This is by far the most common way of dealing with our Shadow, because it offers almost daily release. We cannot admit to ourselves certain desires—for sex, for money, for power, for superiority in some area—and so instead we project those desires onto others.

For instance, we accuse another person in some conflict of having authoritarian desires. In fact, they are simply defending themselves. We are the ones who secretly wish to dominate, but if we see it in the other side first, we can vent our repressed desire in the form of a judgement and justify our own authoritarian response.

Remember: behind any vehement hatred is often a secret and very unpalatable envy of the hated person or people. It is only through such hate that it can be released from the unconscious in some form.

Consider yourself a detective when it comes to piecing together people's Shadow. Through the various signs you pick up, you can fill in the outlines of their repressed desires and impulses. This will allow you to anticipate future leakage and odd Shadow-like behavior.

Rest assured such behavior never occurs just once, and it will tend to pop up in different areas.

We can never alter human nature through enforced niceness. The pitchfork doesn't work. Nor is the solution to seek release for our Shadow in the group, which is volatile and dangerous. Instead the answer is to see our Shadow in action and become more self-aware. It is hard to project onto others our own secret impulses or to overidealize some cause, once we are made aware of the mechanism operating within us. Through such self-knowledge we can find a way to integrate the dark side into our consciousness productively and creatively. In doing so we become more authentic and complete, exploiting to the maximum the energies we naturally possess.

Deciphering the Shadow: Contradictory Behavior

In the course of your life you will come upon people who have very emphatic traits that set them apart and seem to be the source of their strength—unusual confidence, exceptional niceness and affability, great moral rectitude and a saintly aura, toughness and rugged masculinity, and intimidating intellect. If you look closely at them, you may notice a slight exaggeration to these traits, as if they were performing or laying it on just a little too thick. As a student of human nature, you must understand the reality: the emphatic trait generally rests on top of the opposite trait, distracting and concealing it from public view.

Your task is simple: be extra wary around people who display such emphatic traits. It is very easy to get caught up in the appearance and first impression. Watch for the signs and emergence of the opposite over time. It is much easier to deal with such types once you understand them. The following are seven of the most common emphatic traits that you must learn to recognize and manage appropriately.

The Tough Guy: He projects a rough masculinity that is intended to intimidate. Do not be fooled by appearances. Such men have learned to conceal an underlying softness, an emotional vulnerability from deep within that terrifies them.

You must not let yourself be intimidated by the front, but also be careful to not stir up their deep insecurities by seeming to doubt their tall tales or masculine nature. They are notoriously touchy and thin-skinned, and you might detect a micropout on their face if you trigger their insecurities, before they cover it up with a fierce scowl. If they happen to be a rival, they are easy to bait into an overreaction that reveals something less than tough.

The Saint: These people are paragons of goodness and purity. This saintly exterior developed early on as a way to disguise their strong hunger for power and attention or their strong sensual appetites. And once they are in power, the Shadow will have space to operate.

There are genuine saints out there, but they do not feel the need to publicize their deeds or grab power. To distinguish between the real and the fake, ignore their words and the aura they project, focusing on their deeds and the details of their life—how much they seem to enjoy power and attention, the astonishing degree of wealth they have accumulated, the number of mistresses, the level of self-absorption. Once you recognize this type, do not become a naïve follower. Keep some distance. If they are enemies, simply shine a light on the clear signs of hypocrisy.

The Passive-Aggressive Charmer: These types are amazingly nice and accommodating when you first meet them, so much so that you tend to let them into your life rather quickly. Then something ugly occurs—a blowup, some act of sabotage or betrayal—so unlike that nice, charming person you first befriended.

The truth is that these types realize early on in life that they have aggressive, envious tendencies that are hard to control. Over many years they cultivate the opposite façade—their niceness has an almost aggressive edge. Through this stratagem they are able to gain social power.

Your best defense is to be wary of people who are too quick to charm and befriend, too nice and accommodating at first. Keep your distance and look for some early signs, such as passive-aggressive comments. If you notice that—somewhat out of character—they indulge in malicious gossip about someone, you can be sure the

Shadow is speaking and that you will be the target of such gossip one day.

The Fanatic: You are impressed by their fervor, in support of whatever cause. But at the key moment when they could possibly deliver what they have promised, they unexpectedly slip up. They become indecisive at the wrong moment, or burn themselves out and fall ill, or take such ill-conceived actions that it all falls apart.

You will notice in their past some shifts in their belief system, sometimes radical. That is because it is not the particular belief that matters but the intense conviction, and so they will shift this around to fit the times. Belief in something is like a drug for them. But the doubts return. They secretly know they cannot deliver the goods. And so under stress they become the opposite—indecisive and secretly doubtful.

Never be taken in by the strength of people's convictions and their flair for drama. Always operate by the rule that the greater the stridency in what they say, the deeper the underlying insecurities and doubts.

The Rigid Rationalist: All of us have irrational tendencies. We must simply accept this. But for some people, this makes them terribly uncomfortable. They experience primitive thinking as softness, as mysticism, as contrary to science and technology.

The repressed, however, always returns. Their faith in science and technology has a religious air to it. When it comes to an argument, they will impose their ideas with extra intellectual heft and even a touch of anger, which reveals the stirring of the primitive within and the hidden emotional need to bully. They are also prone to strange shifts in mood and emotional outbursts as the Shadow stirs. Bait them into just such overreactions to prick their bubble of intellectual superiority.

The Snob: These types have a tremendous need to be different from others, to assert some form of superiority over the mass of mankind. They put a lot of emphasis on appearances—they are more "alternative" than others, their tattoos are more unique. Of course, it later comes out that they were exaggerating or downright lying about their background.

The truth is that banality is part of human existence. We all have mediocre sides to our character and skills. Snobs are especially sensitive about this, greatly insecure about their origins and possible mediocrity. Their way of dealing with this is to distract and deceive with appearances (as opposed to real originality in their work), surrounding themselves with the extraordinary and with special knowledge.

In any case, those who are truly original and different do not need to make a great show of it. Be extra wary of those who go out of their way to make a show of their difference.

The Extreme Entrepreneur: At first glance these types seem to possess very positive qualities, especially for work. They maintain very high standards and pay exceptional attention to detail. But underneath the façade the seeds of failure are taking root. This first appears is their inability to listen to others. In fact, they mistrust those who do not have their same high standards. With success they are forced to take on more and more responsibility.

If they were truly self-reliant, they would know the importance of delegating on a lower level to maintain control on the higher level, but something else is stirring within—the Shadow. Soon the situation becomes chaotic. Others must come in and take over the business. Their health and finances are ruined and they become completely dependent on doctors or outside financiers. They go from complete control to total dependence on others.

Often their outward show of self-reliance disguises a hidden desire to have others take care of them, to regress to the dependency of childhood. They can never admit to themselves or show any signs of such weakness, but unconsciously they are drawn to creating enough chaos that they break down and are forced into some form of dependency. There are signs beforehand: recurring health issues, the sudden microneeds to be pampered by people in their daily lives. But the big sign comes as they lose control and fail to take steps to halt this. It is best to not get too entangled with such types later on in their careers, as they have a tendency to bring about much collateral damage.

The Integrated Human

In the course of our lives we inevitably meet people who appear to be especially comfortable with themselves. They display certain traits that help give this impression: they are able to laugh at themselves; they can admit to certain shortcomings in their character, as well as to mistakes they have made; they have a playful, sometimes impish edge to them, as if they have retained more of the child within; they can play their role in life with a little bit of distance. At times they can be charmingly spontaneous.

What such people signal to us is a greater authenticity. If most of us have lost a lot of our natural traits in becoming socialized adults, the authentic types have somehow managed to keep them alive and active. We are completely drawn to the authentic types and unconsciously repulsed by their opposite. The reason for this is simple: we all secretly mourn for the child part of our character we have lost—the wildness, the spontaneity, the intensity of experience, the open mind. Our overall energy is diminished by the loss. Those who emit that air of authenticity signal to us another possibility—that of being an adult who has managed to integrate the child and the adult, the dark and the light, the unconscious and the conscious mind. We yearn to be around them. Perhaps some of their energy will rub off on us.

Conscious of our Shadow, we can control, channel, and integrate it. Aware of what we have lost, we can reconnect to that part of ourselves that has sunk into the Shadow.

The following are four clear and practical steps for achieving this.

See the Shadow. The best way to begin is to look for indirect signs, as indicated in the sections above. For instance, take note of any particular one-sided, emphatic traits in yourself. Assume that the opposite trait lies buried deep within, and from there try to see more signs of this trait in your behavior. Look at your own emotional outbursts and moments of extreme touchiness. Your sensitivity to a remark or imputation indicates a Shadow quality that is stirring, in the form of a deep insecurity. Bring it into the light.

Look deeply at your tendencies to project emotions and bad qualities onto people you know, or even entire groups. Look at moments in your youth (late teens, early twenties) in which you acted in a rather insensitive or even cruel manner. When you were younger, you had less control of the Shadow and it came out more naturally, not with the repressed force of later years.

Take this process deeper by reexamining the earlier version of yourself. Look at traits in childhood that were drummed out of you by your parents and peers—certain weaknesses or vulnerabilities or forms of behavior, traits you were made to feel ashamed of. Look at emotions you were once prone to, things that sparked a sense of awe or excitement that has gone missing. You have become more like others as you have gotten older, and you must rediscover the lost authentic parts of yourself.

Finally, look at your dreams as the most direct and

clear view of your Shadow. The Shadow is talking to you in various ways. Don't look for symbols or hidden meanings. Pay attention instead to the emotional tone and overall feelings that they inspire, holding on to them throughout the day. Get in the habit of writing your dreams down and paying deep attention to their feeling tone.

Embrace the Shadow. Your natural reaction in uncovering and facing up to your dark side is to feel uncomfortable and maintain only a surface awareness of it. Your goal here must be the opposite—not only complete acceptance of the Shadow but the desire to integrate it into your present personality.

Explore the Shadow. Consider the Shadow as having depths that contain great creative energy. You want to explore these depths, which include more primitive forms of thinking and the darkest impulses that come out of our animal nature.

The conscious thinking we depend on is quite limited. But the unconscious contains an almost limitless amount of material from memories, experiences, and information absorbed in study. After prolonged research or work on a problem, when we relax our minds in dreams or while we are performing unrelated banal activities, the unconscious begins to go to work and associate all sorts of random ideas, some of the more interesting ones bubbling to the surface. We all have dreams, intuitions, and free associations of ideas, but we often refuse to pay attention to them or take them seriously. Instead you want to develop the habit of using this form of thought more often by having unstructured time in which you can play with ideas, widen the options you consider, and pay serious attention to what comes to you in less conscious states of mind.

In a similar vein, you want to explore from within your own darkest impulses, even those that might seem criminal, and find a way to express them in your work or externalize them in some fashion, in a journal for instance.

Show the Shadow. Most of the time we secretly suffer from the endless social codes we have to adhere to. In following this path we gain comfort by fitting in, but we also become defensive and secretly resentful. At the same time, our Shadow will show itself, but unconsciously, in explosive fits and starts, and often to our detriment.

It would be wise to look at those who are successful in their field. Inevitably we will see that most of them are much less bound by these codes. They are generally more assertive and overtly ambitious. They flout the conventions openly and proudly. And they are not punished but greatly rewarded.

You pay a greater price for being so nice and deferential than for consciously showing your Shadow. First, to follow the latter path you must begin by respecting your own opinions more and those of others less, particularly when it comes to your areas of expertise, to the field you have immersed yourself in. Second, get in the habit in your daily life of asserting yourself more and compromising less. Do this under control and at opportune moments. Third, start caring less what people think of you. Fourth, realize that at times you must offend and even hurt people who block your path, who have ugly values, who unjustly criticize you. Use such moments of clear injustice to bring out your Shadow and show it proudly. Fifth, feel free to play the impudent, willful child who mocks the stupidity and hypocrisy of others.

Finally, flout the very conventions that others follow so scrupulously.

In general, consider this a form of exorcism. Once you show these desires and impulses, they no longer lie hidden in corners of your personality, twisting and operating in secret ways. You have released your demons and enhanced your presence as an authentic human. In this way, the Shadow becomes your ally.

> Unfortunately there is no doubt about the fact that man is, as a whole, less good than he imagines himself or wants to be. Everyone carries a shadow, and the less it is embodied in the individual's conscious life, the blacker and denser it is.
>
> —*Carl Jung*

10

Beware the Fragile Ego

— ✧ —

The Law of Envy

We humans are naturally compelled to compare ourselves with one another. We are continually measuring people's status, the levels of respect and attention they receive, and noticing any difference between what we have and what they have. For some of us, this need to compare serves as a spur to excel through our work. For others, it can turn into deep envy—feelings of inferiority and frustration that lead to covert attacks and sabotage. Nobody admits to acting out of envy. You must recognize the early warning signs—praise and bids for friendship that seem effusive and out of proportion; subtle digs at you under the guise of good-natured humor; apparent uneasiness with your success. It is most likely to crop up among friends or your peers in the same profession. Learn to deflect envy by drawing attention away from yourself. Develop your sense of self-worth from internal standards and not incessant comparisons.

Every time a friend succeeds, I die a little.

—*Gore Vidal*

Keys to Human Nature

Of all the human emotions, none is trickier or more elusive than envy. It is very difficult to actually discern the envy that motivates people's actions or to even know that we have suffered an envy attack from another. This is what makes it so frustrating to deal with and so dangerous.

The reason for this elusiveness is simple: we almost never directly express the envy we are feeling. If we feel anger toward people because of something they said or did, we may try to disguise our anger for various reasons, but we are aware that we are feeling hostile. But envy is very different.

Your task as a student of human nature is to transform yourself into a master decoder of envy. You are ruthless in your analysis and your determination to get to the root of what motivates people. The signs that people emit of envy are harder to discern, but they exist, and you can master the language with some effort and subtle discernment. Think of it as an intellectual challenge.

Before immersing yourself in the subtleties of the emotion, it is important to distinguish between *passive* and *active* envy. All of us in the course of a day will inevitably feel some pangs of envy, as we unconsciously monitor the people around us and sense that they might have more. If these pangs rise to the level of consciousness and are a bit acute, we might say something hurtful or mean-spirited as a way to vent the emotion. But generally as we experience this passive form of envy, we do not do anything that would in any meaningful way harm the relationship with a friend or colleague. In detecting signs of passive envy in others (for instance, little put-downs and offhand comments), you should simply tolerate this as a fact of being a social animal.

Sometimes, however, this passive envy turns active. The underlying sense of inferiority is too strong, leading to hostility that cannot be vented by a comment or put-down.

Your goal is to detect the signs of this more acute form of envy before it turns dangerous. You can do this in three ways: by learning the signs of envy that manage to leak through, by being aware of the types of people who are more prone to acting on envy, and by understanding the circumstances and actions that might trigger active envy in people. You can never see all of the actions motivated by envy; people are simply too good at disguising it. But using all three decoding devices will increase your chances of detection.

Signs of Envy

Although the signs are subtle, envious feelings tend to leak out and can be detected if you are observant. Seeing one such sign in isolation might indicate passive or weak envy. You want to look for combinations or repetitions of the following signs, a pattern, before moving to alert mode.

Microexpressions: When people first experience envy, they have not yet fooled themselves into thinking it is something else, and so they are more prone to leakage than later on. That is why first impressions are often the most accurate and should be given added weight in this case. Envy is most associated with the eyes.

You will notice the envier's eyes momentarily boring into you, with a look that suggests disdain and a touch of hostility. With this look the corners of the mouth will often be turned down, the nose in a sneering, somewhat upturned position, the chin jutting out. Although the look will be a little too direct and held a little too long, it still will not last more than a second or two. It is usually followed with a strained, fake smile. Often you will see the look by accident, as you suddenly turn your head their direction, or you will feel their eyes burning into you without directly looking at them.

If you see such looks in the first few encounters with someone, and they happen more than once, be on the lookout for a dangerous envier entering your life.

Poisonous praise: A major envy attack is often preceded by little envy bites—offhand comments expertly designed to get under your skin. Confusing, paradoxical praise is a common form of this. You feel confused—they have praised you, but in a way that makes you uncomfortable. These comments will also come at moments chosen to cause maximum doubt and damage, for instance just when you have heard the good news and feel a flush of joy.

Poisonous praise almost always indicates envy. They feel the need to praise, but what dominates is the underlying hostility. If they have a habit of praising in this way, if you experience it several times, it is probably an indication of something more intense stirring within them.

Backbiting: If people like to gossip, particularly about common acquaintances, you can be sure they will gossip about you. And gossip is a frequent cover for envy, a convenient way to vent it by sharing malicious rumors and stories.

If you ever get wind of a story they have spread about you, subtly or not so subtly negative, only one such instance should be enough to raise your antennae. What indicates active envy in this case is that they are your friend and they feel the need to vent their underlying hostility to a third party rather than keep it to themselves. In any event, serial gossipers do not make loyal and trustworthy friends.

The push and pull: Enviers often use friendship and intimacy as the best way to wound the people they envy. Through the closeness they establish they are able to gather material on you and find your weak points. Suddenly, after your emotions are engaged, they criticize you in pointed ways. The criticism is confusing, not particularly related to anything you have done, but still you feel guilty. They then return to their initial warmth. You are trapped between the warm friendship and the occasional pain they inflict.

In criticizing you, they are experts at picking out any possible flaws in your character or words you might have regretted, and giving them great emphasis. When you've had enough and decide to defend yourself or criticize them or break off the friendship, they can now ascribe to you a mean or even cruel streak and tell others of this. You will notice in their past other intense relationships with dramatic breakups, always the other person's fault. And at the source of this pattern, something hard to discern, is that they choose to befriend people whom they envy for some quality, then subtly torture them.

In general, criticism of you that seems sincere but not directly related to anything you have actually done is usually a strong sign of envy. People want to bully and overwhelm you with something negative, both wounding you and covering any tracks of envy.

Envier Types

According to the psychoanalyst Melanie Klein (1882 – 1960), certain people are prone to feeling envy their entire lives, and this begins in early infancy. A pattern is set for their entire lives—they are children and later adults for whom nothing is ever quite good enough.

Depending on their psychological makeup, they will tend to conform to certain envying types. It is of great benefit to be able to recognize such types early on, because they are the ones most likely to turn active with their envy. The following are five common varieties of enviers, how they tend to disguise themselves, and their particular forms of attack.

The Leveler: When you first meet them, levelers can seem rather entertaining and interesting. They also seem to have a keen nose for injustice and unfairness in this world. But where they differ from people with genuine empathy for underdogs is that levelers cannot recognize or appreciate excellence in almost anyone, except those who are dead. You will notice that though they can put others down, they do not take easily to any jokes at their expense. They often celebrate low culture and trash, because mediocre work does not stir their insecurities.

Their main goal is to bring everyone down to the same mediocre level they occupy. This sometimes means leveling not only achievers and the powerful but also those who are having too good a time, who seem to be enjoying themselves too much, or who have too great a sense of purpose, which levelers lack.

Be wary around such types, particularly in the workplace, because they will make you feel guilty for your own impulse to excel.

The Self-entitled Slacker: In the world today many people rightfully feel entitled to have success and the good things in life, but they usually understand that this will require sacrifice and hard work. Some people, however, feel they deserve attention and many rewards in life as if these are *naturally* due to them. These self-entitled slackers are generally quite narcissistic. They will make the briefest outline for a novel or screenplay they want to write, or an "idea" for a brilliant business, and feel that that is enough to attract praise and attention. But deep down, these slackers feel insecure about their ability to get what they want; that is why they have never really developed the proper discipline. When they find themselves around high achievers who work very hard and have earned true respect for their work, this will make them aware of the doubts about themselves they have been trying to repress. They will move quickly from envy to hostility.

Be extra careful in the work environment with those who like to maintain their position through charm and being political, rather than by getting things done. They are very prone to envying and hating those who work hard and get results. They will slander and sabotage you without any warning.

The Status Fiend: As social animals we humans are very sensitive to our rank and position within any group. But for some people status is more than a way of measuring social position—it is the most important determinant of their self-worth. You will notice such fiends by the questions they ask about how much money you make, whether you own your home, what kind of neighborhood it's in, whether you occasionally fly business class, and all of the other petty things that they can use as points of comparison. If you are of a higher social status than they are, they will conceal their envy by appearing to admire your success. But if you are a peer or happen to work with them, they will be sniffing for any sign of favoritism or privileges they don't have, and they will attack you in underhanded ways, undermining your position within the group.

Recognize status fiends by how they reduce everything to material considerations. When they comment on the clothes you wear or the car you drive, they seem to focus on the money these things must have cost, and as they talk about such things, you will notice something childish in their demeanor, as if they were reliving a family drama in which they felt cheated by a sibling who had something better. Don't be fooled by their driving an older car or dressing shabbily. These types will often try to assert their status in the opposite direction, by being the consummate monk, the idealistic hippie, while secretly yearning for the luxuries they cannot get through hard work. If you are around such types, try to downplay or conceal what you have that might trigger envy, and talk up their possessions, skills, and status in whatever way you can.

The Attacher: In any court-like environment of power, you will inevitably find people who are drawn to those who are successful or powerful, not out of admiration but out of secret envy. They find a way to attach themselves as friends or assistants. They make themselves useful. They may admire their boss for some qualities, but deep down they believe they are entitled to have some of the attention he or she is getting, without all the hard work. The longer they are around the high achiever, the more this feeling gnaws at them. They have talent, they have dreams—why should the person they work for be so favored? They are good at concealing the undercurrent of envy through excessive fawning. But these types attach themselves because it gives them some kind of satisfaction to spoil and wound the person who has more. They are drawn to the powerful out of a desire to harm them in some way.

In general, be wary of those who are too eager to attach themselves to your life, too impatient to make themselves useful. They try to draw you into a relationship not by their experience and competence but by the flattery and attention they give you. Their form of attack is to gather information on you that they can leak out or spread as gossip, harming your reputation. Learn to hire and work with those who have experience rather than just a pleasing manner.

The Insecure Master: For some people, reaching a high position validates their self-opinion and boosts their self-esteem. But there are some who are more anxious. Holding a high position tends to increase their insecurities, which they are careful to conceal. They look at others who might have more talent, even those below them, with an envious eye.

You will work for such bosses under the assumption they are self-assured and confident. You will work extra hard to impress them, show them you're a person on the way up, only to find yourself after several months suddenly demoted or fired, which makes little sense, since you had clearly delivered results. You did not realize you were dealing with the insecurity variety and had inadvertently triggered their self-doubts.

Pay attention to those above you for signs of insecurity or envy. They will inevitably have a track record of firing people for strange reasons. They will not seem particularly happy with that excellent report you turned in. Always play it safe by deferring to bosses, making them look better, and earning their trust. Couch your brilliant ideas as their ideas. Let them get all the credit for your hard work. Your time to shine will come, but not if you inadvertently stimulate their insecurities.

Envy Triggers

Although certain types are more prone to envy, you must also be aware that there are circumstances that will tend to trigger envy in almost anyone.

The most common trigger is a sudden change in your status, which alters your relationship to friends and peers. This is particularly true among people in your own profession. Do not take so personally their faint praise and veiled criticisms. But be aware that among some of these peers envy can turn active and dangerous.

The best you can do in such situations is to have some self-deprecating humor and to not rub people's faces in your success, which, after all, might contain some element of luck. For those closest to you, offer to help them in their struggles as best you can, without appearing patronizing.

Keep in mind that people who are getting older, with their careers on the decline, have delicate egos and are quite prone to experiencing envy.

If you have any natural gifts that elevate you above others, you must be aware of the dangers and avoid flaunting such talents. Instead you want to strategically reveal some flaws to blunt people's envy and mask your natural superiority. Show your intellectual clumsiness at subjects outside your expertise.

Women who achieve success and fame are more prone to attracting envy and hostility, although this will always be veiled as something else—such women are said to be too cold, or ambitious, or unfeminine. A high-achieving woman inflicts greater feelings of inferiority in both other women and men ("I'm inferior to a woman?"), which leads to envy and hostility, not admiration.

Successful women will have to be even more adept at deflecting envy and playing the humble card.

If you find yourself under an envy attack, your best strategy is to control your emotions. At all costs, maintain your composure. If possible, get some physical distance as well—fire them, cut off contact, whatever is possible. The best strategy is to let them stew in their "cold poison" from a distance, without any future means of wounding you.

Finally, you might imagine that envy is a somewhat

rare occurrence in the modern world. But the truth is that envy is more prevalent now than ever before, largely because of social media. Through social media we have a continual window into the lives of friends, pseudofriends, and celebrities. And what we see is not some unvarnished peek into their world but a highly idealized image that they present.

What we experience in this case is a generalized feeling of dissatisfaction. Low-grade envy sits inside us, waiting to be triggered into the more acute variety if something we read or see intensifies our insecurities.

What this means is simple: we will find more and more people around us prone to feeling passive envy that can turn into the virulent form if we are not careful. We must be prepared to feel its effects coming from friends, colleagues, and the public if we are in the public eye.

Beyond Envy

Like most humans, you will tend to deny that you ever experience envy, at least strong enough to act on. Let us be realistic, however, and realize that it is almost impossible to rid ourselves of the compulsion to compare ourselves with others. It is too ingrained in our nature as a social animal. Instead, what we must aspire to is to slowly transform our comparing inclination into something positive, productive, and prosocial. The following are five simple exercises to help you in achieving this.

Move closer to what you envy. Envy thrives on relative closeness—in a corporate environment where people see each other every day, in a family, in a neighborhood, in any group of peers. But nothing is ever so perfect as it seems, and often we would see that we are mistaken if we only looked closely enough. Spend time with that family you envy and wish you had as your own, and you will begin to reassess your opinion.

The process of moving closer is twofold: on the one hand, try to actually look behind the glittering facades people present, and on the other hand, simply imagine the inevitable disadvantages that go along with their position.

Engage in downward comparisons: You normally focus on those who seem to have more than you, but it would be wiser to look at those who have less. This should stimulate not only empathy for the many who have less but also greater gratitude for what you actually possess. Such gratitude is the best antidote to envy.

As a related exercise, you can write up all the positive things in your life that you tend to take for granted.

Practice *Mitfreude*. Schadenfreude, the experience of pleasure in the pain of other people, is distinctly related to envy, as several studies have demonstrated. But it would be wise to practice instead the opposite, what the philosopher Friedrich Nietzsche called *Mitfreude*— "joying with."

This means that instead of merely congratulating people on their good fortune, something easy to do and easily forgotten, you must instead actively try to feel their joy, as a form of empathy. Because it is such a rare occurrence, it contains great power to bond people. And in internalizing other people's joy, we increase our own capacity to feel this emotion in relation to our own experiences.

Transmute envy into emulation. We cannot stop the comparing mechanism in our brains, so it is best to redirect it into something productive and creative. Instead of wanting to hurt or steal from the person who has achieved more, we should desire to raise ourselves up to his or her level.

To make this work requires a few psychological shifts. First, we must come to believe that we have the capacity to raise ourselves up. Second, we must develop a solid work ethic to back this up. If we are rigorous and persistent, we will be able to overcome almost any obstacle and elevate our position.

Related to this, having a sense of purpose, a feel for your calling in life, is a great way to immunize yourself against envy.

Admire human greatness. Admiration is the polar opposite of envy—we are acknowledging people's achievements, celebrating them, without having to feel insecure. In recognizing the greatness of someone, we are celebrating the high potential of our species. Such admiration elevates us above the pettiness of our day-to-day life and will have a calming effect.

Finally, it is worth cultivating moments in life in which we feel immense satisfaction and happiness divorced from our own success or achievements. These are sublime moments, and as far removed from the pettiness and poisons of envy as possible.

> For not many men ... can love a friend who fortune prospers
> without envying; and about the envious brain
> cold poison clings and doubles all the pain
> life brings him. His own woundings he must nurse,
> and feel another's gladness like a curse.
>
> *—Aeschylus*

11

Know Your Limits

———— ◇ ————

The Law of Grandiosity

We humans have a deep need to think highly of ourselves. If that opinion of our goodness, greatness, and brilliance diverges enough from reality, we become grandiose. We imagine our superiority. Often a small measure of success will elevate our natural grandiosity to even more dangerous levels. Our high self-opinion has now been confirmed by events. We forget the role that luck may have played in the success, or the contributions of others. We imagine we have the golden touch. Losing contact with reality, we make irrational decisions. That is why our success often does not last. Look for the signs of elevated grandiosity in yourself and in others—overbearing certainty in the positive outcome of your plans; excessive touchiness if criticized; a disdain for any form of authority. Counteract the pull of grandiosity by maintaining a realist assessment of yourself and your limits. Tie any feelings of greatness to your work, your achievements, and your contributions to society.

Existence alone had never been enough for him;
he had always wanted more. Perhaps it was only

from the force of his desires that he had regarded himself as a man to whom more was permitted than to others.

–*Fyodor Dostoyevsky,* Crime and Punishment

Keys to Human Nature

Let us say that you have a project to realize, or an individual or group of people you wish to persuade to do something. You can think of the project or task ahead of you as a block of marble you must sculpt into something precise and beautiful. The block is much larger than you and the material is quite resistant, but the task is not impossible. With enough effort, focus, and resiliency you can slowly carve it into what you need. You must begin, however, with a proper sense of proportion—goals are hard to reach, people are resistant, and you have limits to what you can do. With such a realistic attitude, you can summon up the requisite patience and get to work.

Imagine, however, that your brain has succumbed to a psychological disease that affects your perception of size and proportion. Instead of seeing the task you are facing as rather large and the material resistant, under the influence of this disease you perceive the block of marble as relatively small and malleable. Losing your sense of proportion, you believe it won't take long to fashion the block into the image you have in your mind of the finished product. You imagine that the people you are trying to reach are not naturally resistant but quite predictable. The emphasis is not on what you need to do to succeed but on what you feel you deserve.

We can call this psychological disease *grandiosity*. As you feel its effects, the normal realist proportions are reversed—your self becomes larger and greater than anything else around it. That is the lens through which you view the task and the people you need to reach. This is not merely narcissism, in which everything must revolve around you. It is a feeling of being not merely human but godlike.

Your task as a student of human nature is threefold: First, you must understand the phenomenon of grandiosity itself, why it is so embedded in human nature, and why you will find many more grandiose people in the world today than ever before. Second, you need to recognize the signs of grandiosity and know how to manage the people who display them. And third and most important, you must see the signs of the disease in yourself and learn not only how to control your grandiose tendencies but also how to channel this energy into something productive.

Grandiosity has its roots in the earliest years of our life. In our first months, most of us bonded completely with our mother. We came to believe that the breast that gave us food was actually a part of ourselves. We were omnipotent—all we had to do was feel hungry or feel any need, and the mother was there to meet it, as if we had magical powers to control her. But then, slowly, we had to go through a second phase of life in which we were forced to confront the reality—our mother was a separate being who had other people to attend to. We were not omnipotent but rather weak, quite small, and dependent. This realization was painful and the source of much of our acting out—we had a deep need to assert ourselves, to show we were not so helpless, and to fantasize about powers we did not possess.

Some children do not go through that second phase in early childhood in which they must confront their relative smallness, and these children are more vulnerable to deeper forms of grandiosity later in life. They are the pampered, spoiled ones. The mother and the father continue to make such children feel like they are the center of the universe, shielding them from the pain of confronting the reality.

The early pampering marks them for life. They need to be adored. They become masters at manipulating others to pamper them and shower them with attention. They naturally feel greater than anyone above them. If they have any talent, they might rise quite far, as their sense of being born with a crown on their head becomes a self-fulfilling prophecy.

In the past, we humans were able to channel our grandiose needs into religion. Gods and spirits represented these elemental powers of nature that dwarfed our own. By worshipping them we could gain their protection. Connected to something much larger than ourselves, we felt enlarged. Many centuries later, in a similar manner, we channeled this energy into worshipping leaders who represented a great cause and promoted a future utopia, such as Napoleon Bonaparte and the French Revolution.

Today, in the Western world, religions and great causes have lost their binding power; we find it hard to believe in them and to satisfy our grandiose energy through identification with a greater power. The need to feel larger and significant, however, does not simply disappear; it is stronger than ever. And absent any other channels, people will tend to direct this energy toward themselves. Because of this, we find more and more grandiose individuals among us.

Other factors have also contributed to increases in grandiosity. First, we find more people who experienced pampering attention in their childhood than ever in the past. Second, we find increasing numbers of people who have little or no respect for authority or experts of any kind, no matter the experts' level of training and experience, which they themselves lack. Without a sense of anyone rightly being above them and deserving authority, they can position themselves among the highest.

Third, technology gives us the impression that everything in life can be as fast and simple as the information we can glean online. It instills the belief that we no longer have to spend years learning a skill; instead, through a few tricks and with a few hours a week of practice we can become proficient at anything. But more than anything it is social media that spreads the grandiosity virus. Through social media we have almost limitless powers to expand our presence, to create the illusion that we have the attention and even adoration of thousands or millions of people.

With all of these elements combined, it is harder than ever for any of us to maintain a realistic attitude and a proportionate sense of self.

In looking at the people around you, you must realize that their grandiosity (and yours) can come in many different forms. Most commonly people will try to satisfy the need by gaining social prestige. People may claim they are interested in the work itself or in contributing to humanity, but often deep down what is really motivating them is the desire to have attention, to have their high self-opinion confirmed by others who admire them, to feel powerful and inflated.

People still tend to idealize leaders and worship them, and you must see this as a form of grandiosity. By believing someone else will make everything great, followers can feel something of this greatness. On a more personal level, people will often idealize those they love, elevating them to god or goddess status and by extension feeling some of this power reflected back on them.

In the world today, you will also notice the prevalence of negative forms of grandiosity. Many people feel the need to disguise their grandiose urges not only from others but also from themselves. They will frequently make a show of their humility—they are not interested in power or feeling important, or so they say. But you will notice they have a need to display this humility in a public manner. It is grandiose humility—their way to get attention and to feel morally superior.

A variation on this is the *grandiose victim*—they have suffered a lot and been the victim numerous times. In essence, they are compelled to create the drama that will turn them into a victim. Feeling and expressing their misfortune gives them their sense of importance, of being superior in suffering.

You can measure the levels of grandiosity in people in several simple ways. For instance, notice how people respond to criticism of them or their work. Some people become enraged and hysterical, because we have called into doubt their sense of greatness. You can be sure that such a person has high levels of grandiosity. Similarly, such types might conceal their rage behind a martyred, pained expression meant to make you feel guilty.

Grandiose people are generally big talkers. They take credit for anything that is even tangential to their work; they invent past successes. Higher grandiose types generally display low levels of empathy. They are not good listeners. When the attention is not on them, they have a faraway look in their eyes and their fingers twitch with impatience. Finally, they exhibit nonverbal behavior that can only be described as grandiose. Their gestures are big and dramatic. Their voice tends to be louder than others, and they speak at a fast pace, giving no one else time to interrupt.

If such types happen to be your rivals, consider yourself lucky. They are easy to taunt and bait into overreactions.

Finally, you will need to manage your own grandiose tendencies. The greatest protection you can have against grandiosity is to maintain a realistic attitude. You know what subjects and activities you are naturally attracted to. You need to play to your strengths and not imagine you can be great at whatever you put your mind to. You must have a thorough understanding of your energy levels, of how far you can reasonably push yourself, and of how this changes with age.

This self-awareness has a physical component to it that you must be sensitive to. When you are doing activities that mesh with your natural inclinations, you feel ease in the effort. When you take on too much, more than you can handle, you feel not only exhausted but also irritable and nervous. You are prone to headaches. When you have success in life, you will naturally feel a touch of fear, as if the good fortune could disappear. You sense with this fear the dangers that can come from rising too high and feeling too superior. Your anxiety is telling you to come back down to earth.

The Grandiose Leader

If people with high levels of grandiosity also possess some talent and a lot of assertive energy, they can rise to positions of great power. Mesmerized by their image, we often fail to see the underlying irrationality in their decision-making process and so follow them straight into some disaster. They can be very destructive.

To awe us and distract us from the reality, they employ certain theatrical devices. It is imperative for us to see through their stage tricks, to demythologize them and scale them back down to human size. The following are six common illusions they like to create.

I am destined. Grandiose leaders often try to give the impression that they were somehow destined for greatness. They tell stories of their childhood and youth that indicate their uniqueness, as if fate had singled them out. They highlight events that showed from early on their unusual toughness or creativity, either making such stories up or reinterpreting the past. The future great leader was already in gestation at a young age, or so they make it seem. When you hear such things you must become skeptical. Look for the more mundane facts behind the tales of destiny and, if possible, publicize them.

I'm the common man/woman. In some cases grandiose leaders may have risen from the lower classes, but in general they either come from relatively privileged backgrounds or because of their success have lived removed from the cares of everyday people for quite some time. Nevertheless it is absolutely essential to present themselves to the public as highly representative of the average man and woman out there. Only through such a presentation can they attract the attention and the adoration of large enough numbers to satisfy themselves.

The trick grandiose leaders play is to place the emphasis on their cultural tastes, not on the actual class they come from. The public can now identify with them despite the obvious contradictions. But the grandiosity of this goes beyond merely gaining more attention. These leaders become vastly enlarged by this identification with the masses. They are not merely one man or woman but embody an entire nation or interest group. To criticize them is to want to crucify the leader and betray the cause.

If you notice such paradoxes and primitive forms of popular association, stand back and analyze the reality of what is going on.

I will deliver you. These types often rise to power in times of trouble and crisis. They will be the ones to deliver the people from the many problems they are facing. In order to pull this off, their promises have to be large yet vague. The message must be simple to digest, reducible to a slogan, and promising something large that stirs the emotions.

What you will find here is that they are creating a cult more than leading a political movement or a business. You will see that their name, image, and slogans must be reproduced in large numbers and assume a godlike ubiquity. People who now believe in the cult are doubly mesmerized and ready to excuse any kind of action. At such a point nothing will dissuade true believers, but you must maintain your internal distance and analytic powers.

I rewrite the rules. A secret wish of humans is to do without the usual rules and conventions in place in any field—to gain power just by following our own inner light. When grandiose leaders claim to have such powers, we are secretly excited and wish to believe them.

As a variation on this, grandiose leaders will often rely on their intuitions, disregarding the need for focus groups or any form of scientific feedback. They like to create the myth that their hunches have led to fantastic successes, but close scrutiny will reveal that their hunches miss as often as they hit. When you hear leaders present themselves as the consummate maverick, able to do away with rules and science, you must see this only as a sign of madness, not divine inspiration.

I have the golden touch. Those with heightened grandiosity will try to create the legend that they have never really failed. If there were failures or setbacks in their career, it was always the fault of others who betrayed them. Related to this is the belief that they can easily transfer their skills. This is often a fatal move on their part, as they attempt things beyond their expertise and quickly become overwhelmed with the complexity and chaos that come from their lack of experience. In dealing with such types, look carefully at their record and notice how many glaring failures they have had. Although people under the influence of their grandiosity will probably not listen, publicize the truth of their record in as neutral a manner as possible.

I'm vulnerable. The grandiose leader takes risks. But this boldness is not really under control. These daring activities make them feel alive and on edge. It becomes a drug. They need bigger stakes and rewards to maintain the feeling of godlike invulnerability.

In fact they *are* rather invulnerable, until that fatal hubristic maneuver in which they finally go too far and it all crashes down. Suddenly the aura of being invulnerable is shattered. This occurs because their decisions are determined not by rational considerations but by the need for attention and glory, and eventually reality catches up, in one hard blow.

Practical Grandiosity

Grandiosity is a form of primal energy we all possess. Normally grandiosity makes us imagine we are greater and more superior than is actually the case. We can call this *fantastical grandiosity* because it is based on our fantasies and the skewed impression we get from any attention we receive. The other form, which we shall call *practical grandiosity*, is not easy to achieve and does not come naturally to us, but it can be the source of tremendous power and self-fulfilment.

Practical grandiosity is based not on fantasy but on reality. The energy is channeled into our work and our desire to achieve our goals, to solve problems, or to improve relationships.

Although the precise way to channel the energy will depend on your field and skill level, the following are five basic principles that are essential for attaining the high level of fulfillment that can come from this reality-based form of grandiosity.

Come to terms with your grandiose needs. You need to begin from a position of honesty. You must admit to yourself that you do want to feel important and be the center of attention. Only with this self-awareness can you begin to transform the energy into something practical and productive.

Concentrate the energy. Fantastical grandiosity will make you flit from one fantastic idea to another, imagining all the accolades and attention you'll receive but never realizing any of them. You must do the opposite. You want to get into the habit of focusing deeply and completely on a single project or problem. You want the goal to be relatively simple to reach, and within a time frame of months and not years. You will want to break this down into mini steps and goals along the way. Your objective here is to enter a state of flow, in which your mind becomes increasingly absorbed in the work, to the point at which ideas come to you at odd hours. This feeling of flow should be pleasurable and addicting.

Related to this, you want this project to involve skills you already have or are in the process of developing. Your goal is to see continual improvement in your skill level, which will certainly come from the depth of your focus. Your confidence will rise. That should be enough to keep you advancing.

Maintain a dialogue with reality. Your project begins with an idea, and as you try to hone this idea, you let your imagination take flight, being open to various possibilities. At some point you move from the planning phase to execution. Now you must actively search for feedback and criticism from people you respect or from your natural audience. You want to hear about the flaws and inadequacies in your plan, for that is the only way to improve your skills. If the project fails to have the results you imagined, or the problem is not solved, embrace this as the best way to learn. Analyze what you did wrong in depth, being as brutal as possible.

Once you have feedback and have analyzed the results, you then return to this project or start a new one, letting your imagination loose again but incorporating what you have learned from the experience. By maintaining a continual dialogue between reality (feedback) and your imagination, you will create something practical and powerful.

If you have any success with your projects, that is when you must step back from the attention you are receiving. Look at the role that luck may have played, or the help you received from others. As you now focus on the next idea, see yourself back at square one. Never rest on your laurels or let up in your intensity.

Seek out calibrated challenges. Your goal with practical grandiosity is to continually look for challenges just above your skill level. If the projects you attempt are below or at your skill level, you will become easily bored and less focused. If they are too ambitious, you will feel crushed by your failure. However, if they are calibrated to be more challenging than the last project, but to a moderate degree, you will find yourself excited and energized.

Let loose your grandiose energy. Once you have tamed this energy, made it serve your ambitions and goals, you should feel safe to let it loose upon occasion. Think of it as a wild animal that needs to roam free now and then or it will go mad from restlessness. What this means is that you occasionally allow yourself to entertain ideas or projects that represent greater challenges than you have considered in the past. You feel increasingly confident and you want to test yourself. Consider developing a new skill in an unrelated field, or writing that novel you once considered a distraction from the real work. Or simply give freer rein to your imagination when in the planning process.

> Then, overwhelmed by the afflictions I suffered in connection with my sons, I sent again and inquired of the god what I should do to pass the rest of my life most happily; and he answered me: "Knowing thyself, O Croesus—thus shall you live and be happy" ... [But] spoiled by the wealth I had and by those who were begging me to become their leader, by the gifts they gave me and by the people who flattered me, saying that if I would consent to take command they would all obey me and I should

be the greatest of men—puffed up by such words, when all the princes round about chose me to be their leader in the war, I accepted the command, deeming myself fit to be the greatest; but, as it seems, I did not know myself. For I thought I was capable of carrying on war against you; but I was no match for you ... Therefore, as I was thus without knowledge, I have my just deserts.

—*Xenophon*, The Education of Cyrus

12

Reconnect to the Masculine or Feminine Within You

——— ◇ ———

The Law of Gender Rigidity

All of us have masculine and feminine qualities–some of this is genetic, and some of it comes from the profound influence of the parent of the opposite sex. But in the need to present a consistent identity in society, we tend to repress these qualities, overidentifying with the masculine or feminine role expected of us. And we pay a price for this. We lose valuable dimensions to our character. Our thinking and ways of acting become rigid. Our relationships with members of the opposite sex suffer as we project onto them our own fantasies and hostilities. You must become aware of these lost masculine or feminine traits and slowly reconnect to them, unleashing creative powers in the process. You will become more fluid in your thinking. In bringing out the masculine or feminine undertone to your character, you will fascinate people by being authentically yourself. Do not play the expected gender role, but rather create the one that suits you.

It is the terrible deception of love that it begins
by engaging us in play not with a woman of the
external world but with a doll fashioned in our
brain—the only woman moreover that we have
always at our disposal, the only one we shall ever
possess.

—Marcel Proust

Keys to Human Nature

When in love, we become prey to emotions we cannot
control. We make choices of partners we cannot rationally explain, and often these choices end up being
unfortunate. And often we repeat the same types of
bad choices of partners, as if compelled by some inner
demon.

We like to tell ourselves in retrospect that when we
were in love, a type of temporary madness overcame us.
We think of such moments as representing the excep-
tion, not the rule, to our character. But let us entertain
for the moment the opposite possibility—in our conscious day-to-day life, we are sleep-walking, unaware of
who we really are; we present a front of reasonableness
to the world, and we mistake the mask for reality. When
we fall in love, we are actually being *more* ourselves. We
are more connected to the reality of the essential irrationality in our nature.

In looking at these altered states, we might be
tempted to describe them as forms of possession. We

are normally rational person A, but under the influence of an infatuation, irrational person B begins to emerge. At first, A and B can fluctuate and even blend into each other, but the deeper we fall in love, the more it is person B who dominates. Person B sees qualities in people that are not there, acts in ways that are counterproductive and even self-destructive, is quite immature, with unrealistic expectations, and makes decisions that are often mysterious later on to person A.

When it comes to our behavior in these situations, we never really completely understand what is happening. But the eminent psychologist Carl Jung—who analyzed over the course of his very long career thousands of men and women with stories of painful love affairs—offered perhaps the most profound explanation for what happens to us when we fall in love. According to Jung, we *are* actually possessed in such moments. He gave the entity (person B) that takes hold of us the name *anima* (for the male) and *animus* (for the female). This entity exists in our unconscious but comes to the surface when a person of the opposite sex fascinates us.

The unconscious feminine part of the boy and the man is what Jung calls the *anima*. The unconscious masculine part of the girl and woman is the *animus*. Once we become fascinated with a person of the opposite sex, the anima and animus stir to life. The attraction we feel toward another might be purely physical, but more often the person who draws our attention unconsciously bears some resemblance—physical or psychological— to our mother or father. Remember that this primal relationship is full of charged energy, excitement, and obsessions that are repressed but yearning to come out. A person who triggers these associations in us will be a magnet for our attention, even though we are not aware of the source of our attraction.

Because we are not really relating to women and men as they are, but rather to our projections, we will eventually feel disappointed in them as if they are to blame for not being what we had imagined. The relationship will often tend to fall apart from the misreading and miscommunications on both sides, and not aware of the source of this, we will go through precisely the same cycle with the next person.

Your task as a student of human nature is threefold: First you must try to observe the anima and the animus as they manifest themselves in others, particularly in their intimate relationships. By paying attention to their behavior and patterns in these situations, you will have access to their unconscious that is normally denied to you. Pay special attention to those who are hypermasculine or hyperfeminine. You can be sure that below the surface lurks a very feminine anima for the man and a very masculine animus for the woman.

Your second task is to become aware of the projecting mechanism within yourself. Projections have a positive role to play in your life, and you could not stop them even if you wanted to, because they are so automatic and unconscious. But once the relationship develops, you need to have the power and awareness to withdraw the projections, so that you can begin to see women and men as they really are. In doing so, perhaps you will realize how truly incompatible you are, or the opposite. Once connected to the real person, you can continue to idealize him or her, but this will be based on actual positive qualities he or she possesses. You can accomplish all of this by becoming aware of your own patterns and the types of qualities you tend to project onto others.

Your third task is to look inward, to see those feminine or masculine qualities that are repressed and undeveloped within you. That assertiveness you desire to see in a man, or empathy in a woman, is something you need to develop within yourself, bringing out that feminine or masculine undertone. What you are doing in essence is integrating into your everyday personality the traits that are within you but are repressed. They will become part of your everyday self, and people will be drawn to the authenticity they sense in you.

Gender Projection—Types

Although there are infinite variations, below you will find six of the more common types of gender projections. You must use this knowledge in three ways: First, you must recognize in yourself any tendency toward one of these forms of projection. Second, you must use this as an invaluable tool for gaining access to the unconscious of other people, to seeing their anima and animus in action. And finally, you must be attentive to how others will project onto you their needs and fantasies. Better to be aware of this dynamic before it entraps you.

The Devilish Romantic: For the woman in this scenario, the man who fascinates her—often older and successful—might seem like a rake, the type who cannot help but chase after young women. But he is also a romantic. She decides she will seduce him and become the target of his attention. But somehow he is not as strong, masculine, or romantic as she had imagined. She does not get the desired attention, or it does not last very long. He cannot be reformed, and leaves her.

This is often the projection of women who had rather intense, even flirtatious relationships with the father. It becomes her lifelong goal to recapture this attention and the power that goes with it. Any association with the father figure will spark the projecting mechanism, and she will invent or exaggerate the man's romantic nature.

Women in this scenario have become trapped by the early attention paid to them by the father. They have to be continually charming, inspiring, and flirtatious to elicit that attention later on. Their animus is seductive, but with an aggressive, masculine edge, having absorbed so much of the father's energy. The only way out of the trap for such women is to see the pattern itself, to stop mythologizing the father, and to focus instead on the damage he has caused by the inappropriate attention he paid to them.

The Elusive Woman of Perfection: He thinks he

has found the ideal woman. Although he has had few actual encounters with the woman in question, he can imagine all kinds of positive experiences with her. When he talks of this perfect woman, you will notice there's not a lot of concrete detail about what makes her so perfect. If he does manage to forge a relationship, he will quickly become disenchanted. She's not who he thought she was; she misled him. He then moves on to the next woman to project his fantasy onto.

The men prone to this projection often had mothers who were not totally there for them. Perhaps such a mother expected the son to give *her* the attention and validation she was not getting from her husband. Because of this reversal, when the boy becomes a man, he feels a great emptiness inside that he constantly needs to fill. He cannot exactly verbalize what he wants or what he missed, hence the vagueness of his fantasy. His own anima is a bit dreamy, introspective, and moody, which is the behavior he will tend to exhibit when in love.

Men of this type must recognize the nature of their pattern. What they really need is to find and interact with a real woman, accept her inevitable flaws, and give more of themselves. They are too alienated from their own feminine spirit and need to loosen up their own thought processes.

The Lovable Rebel: For the woman who is drawn to this type, the man who intrigues her has a noticeable disdain for authority. Unlike the Devilish Romantic, this man will often be young and not so successful. He will also tend to be outside her usual circle of acquaintances. To have a relationship with him would be ever so slightly taboo. If a relationship does ensue, however, she will see a totally different side to him. Despite the tattoos and shaved head, he's quite conventional, controlling, and domineering. The relationship will break apart, but the fantasy will remain.

The woman with this projection often had a strong, patriarchal father who was distant and strict. As a girl she dreamed of rebelling and asserting herself against the father's control, but too often she was reduced to obeying and playing the deferential daughter. Her desire to rebel was repressed and went into her animus, which is quite angry and resentful. Instead of developing the rebelliousness herself, she looks to externalize it in the form of the rebellious male. Oftentimes she chooses a man who is relatively young because this makes him less threatening, less of a patriarch. But his youth and immaturity make it almost impossible to form a stable relationship, and her angry side will come out as she grows disenchanted.

Once a woman recognizes she is prone to this projection, she must come to terms with a simple fact: what she really wants is to develop the independence, assertiveness, and power to disobey in herself.

The Fallen Woman: To the man in question, the woman who fascinates him seems so different from those he has known. Perhaps she comes from a different culture or social class. Perhaps she is not as educated as he is. There might be something dubious about her character and her past. She seems to be in need of protection, education, and money. He will be the one to rescue and elevate her. But somehow the closer he gets to her, the less it turns out as he had expected.

Men of this type often had strong mother figures in their childhood. They became good, obedient boys, excellent students at school. But unconsciously they are drawn to women who are imperfect, bad, of dubious character. They have repressed the playful, sensual, and earthy sides of the character they had as boys. They are too rigid and civilized. The only way they can relate to these qualities is through women who appear to be so different from themselves. They project onto such women weakness and vulnerability. They tell themselves they want to help and protect them. But what really attracts them is the danger and naughty pleasures these women seem to promise. Underestimating the strength of such women, they often end up as their pawns. Their anima is passive and masochistic.

Men who engage in this kind of projection need to develop the less conventional sides of their character. Not having to get what they crave by looking for the Fallen Woman type, they can actually begin to satisfy their urges with any type of woman, not passively waiting for her to lead them astray but actively initiating the guilty pleasures.

The Superior Man: He seems brilliant, skilled, strong, and stable. He radiates confidence and power.

He could be a high-powered businessman, a professor, an artist, a guru. Even though he may be older and not so physically attractive, his self-assurance gives him an attractive aura. For the woman attracted to this type, a relationship with him would give her an indirect feeling of strength and superiority.

This type of projection is all too common among women. It stems from feelings of inferiority. Not having ever developed her own strength or confidence, she will tend to search for these qualities in men and exaggerate any traces of them. Many of the men who respond to her like the adoring attention of a woman, often younger, whom they can lord over and control. This would be the classic professor seducing the student. Because such men are rarely as brilliant, clever, and self-assured as she imagines, the woman either is disappointed and leaves or is trapped in her low self-esteem, bending to his manipulations and blaming herself for any problems.

What such a woman needs to do is first realize that the source of her insecurity is the critical opinions of others, which she has accepted and internalized. She must actively work at developing her assertiveness and self-confidence through her actions—taking on projects, starting a business, mastering a craft. With genuine self-confidence she will then be able to gauge the true worth and character of the men she meets.

The Woman to Worship Him: He's driven and ambitious, but his life is hard. He feels something missing in his life. Then along comes a woman who is attentive to him, warm, and engaging. She seems to admire him. This is the woman to complete him, to help comfort him. But then, as the relationship develops, she no longer seems quite so nice and attentive. She certainly has stopped admiring him. He concludes that she has deceived him or has changed. Such a betrayal makes him angry.

This male projection generally stems from a particular type of relationship with the mother—she adores her son and showers him with attention. She fills the boy with confidence; he becomes addicted to her attention and craves her warm, enveloping presence, which is what she wants.

When he grows up, he is often quite ambitious, always trying to live up to the expectations of his mother. He chooses a certain type of woman to pursue and then subtly positions her to play the mother role—to comfort, adore, and pump up his ego. In many instances, the woman will come to understand how he has manipulated her into this role, and she will resent it. The ensuing breakup will be very painful for the man, because he has invested energy from his earliest years and will feel this as abandonment from the mother figure.

The man in this case must see the pattern of these relationships in his life. What this should signal to him is that he needs to develop from within more of the mothering qualities that he projects onto women. He needs to be able to care for himself.

The Original Man/Woman

A common experience for us humans is that at a certain point in life—often near the age of forty—we go through what is known as a midlife crisis. We crave change, and we look for it through a new career or relationship, some new experiences, even some danger. Such changes may give us a short-term therapeutic jolt, but they leave the real source of the problem untouched, and the malaise will return.

Let us look at this phenomenon from a different angle—as a crisis of identity. As children, we had a rather fluid sense of self. But in our youth we had to shape a social self, one that was cohesive and would allow us to fit into a group. To do so we had to trim and tighten up our freer-flowing spirit. And much of this tightening revolved around gender roles. We had to repress masculine or feminine aspects of ourselves, in order to feel and present a more consistent self.

But as the years go by, the gender role we play gets more and more fixed, and we begin to sense that we have lost something essential, that we are almost strangers to who we were in our youth. We have become imbalanced, too rigidly identified with our role and the mask we present to others. Our original nature incorporated more of the qualities that we absorbed from the mother or father, and of the traits of the opposite sex that are biologically a part of us.

The return to your original nature contains elemental power. By relating more to the natural feminine or masculine parts within you, you will unleash energy that has been repressed; your mind will recover its natural fluidity; and by ridding yourself of the defensiveness you have in relation to your gender role, you will feel secure in who you are. This return requires that you play with styles of thinking and acting that are more masculine or feminine, depending on your imbalance.

Masculine and feminine styles of thinking: Masculine thinking tends toward focusing on what separates phenomena from one another and categorizing them. It looks for contrasts between things to better label them. It wants to take things apart, like a machine, and analyze the separate parts that go into the whole.

Feminine thinking orients itself differently. It likes to focus on the whole, how the parts connect to one another, the overall gestalt. In looking at a group of people, it wants to see how they relate to one another. Instead of freezing phenomena in time in order to examine them, it focuses on the organic process itself, how one thing grows into another.

Almost all people will lean more toward one style of thinking. What you want for yourself is to create balance by leaning more in the other direction. If you are more on the masculine side, you want to widen the fields you look at, finding connections between different forms of knowledge. If you lean more in the feminine direction, you need to be capable of focusing and digging into specific problems, tamping down the impulse to widen your search and multitask.

Masculine and feminine styles of action: When it comes to taking action, the masculine tendency is to move forward, explore the situation, attack, and vanquish. If there are obstacles in the way, it will try to push through them. It derives pleasure from staying on the offensive and taking risks.

When confronted with a problem or the need to take action, the feminine style often prefers to first withdraw from the immediate situation and contemplate more deeply the options. It will often look for ways to avoid the conflict, to smooth out relations, to win without having to go to battle.

For those with the aggressive, masculine inclination, balance would come from training yourself to step back before taking any action. For those with the feminine style, it is best to accustom yourself to various degrees of conflict and confrontation, so that any avoidance of it is strategic and not out of fear.

Masculine and feminine styles of self-assessment and learning: As studies have shown, when men make mistakes they tend to look outward and find other people or circumstances to blame. On the other hand, men will tend to feel that they are completely responsible for any success in life. For women, it is the opposite: When there is failure, they tend to blame themselves and look inward.

For those with the masculine style, when it comes to learning and improving yourself, it is best to reverse the order—to look inward when you make mistakes and to look outward when you have success. For those with the feminine style, it is easy to beat yourself up after failures or mistakes. The introspection can go too far. You need to adopt more of the masculine self-confidence, without the attendant stupidity.

Masculine and feminine styles of relating to people and leadership: As with male chimpanzees, in a group setting the masculine style is to require a leader, and to either aspire to that role or gain power by being the most loyal follower. Men are highly status conscious, hyperaware of their place in the group. The masculine style of leadership is to identify clear goals and reach them. It puts emphasis on results, however they are achieved.

The feminine style is more about maintaining the group spirit and keeping the relationships smoothed out, with fewer differences among individuals. Results are important, but the way they are achieved, the process is equally important.

For those with the masculine style, it is important to enlarge your concept of leadership. When you think more deeply about the individuals on the team and strategize to involve them more, you can have superior results, engaging the energy and creativity of the group.

For those with the feminine style, you must not be afraid of assuming a strong leadership role, particularly in times of crisis. Although women are certainly better listeners, sometimes it is best to know when to stop listening and go with the plan you have opted for.

What is most beautiful in virile men is something feminine; what is most beautiful in feminine women is something masculine.

—*Susan Sontag*

13

Advance with a Sense of Purpose

— ✧ —

The Law of Aimlessness

Unlike animals, with their instincts to guide them past dangers, we humans have to rely upon our conscious decisions. We do the best we can when it comes to our career path and handling the inevitable setbacks in life. But in the back of our minds we can sense an overall lack of direction, as we are pulled this way and that way by our moods and by the opinions of others. How did we end up in this job, in this place? Such drifting can lead to dead ends. The way to avoid such a fate is to develop a sense of purpose, discovering our calling in life and using such knowledge to guide us in our decisions. We come to know ourselves more deeply—our tastes and inclinations. We trust ourselves, knowing which battles and detours to avoid. Even our moments of doubt, even our failures have a purpose—to toughen us up. With such energy and direction, our actions have unstoppable force.

He who has a why to live can bear with almost any how.

—*Friedrich Nietzsche*

Keys to Human Nature

In the not-so-distant past, people's career and life choices were somewhat limited. They would settle into the particular jobs or roles available to them and stay there for decades. Certain older figures—mentors, family members, religious leaders—could offer some direction if needed. But such stability and help is hard to find today, as the world changes ever more quickly. Everyone is caught up in the harsh struggle to make it; people have never been so preoccupied with their own needs and agendas. The advice of our parents might be totally antiquated in this new order. Facing this unprecedented state of affairs, we tend to react in one of two ways.

Some of us, excited by all the changes, actually embrace this new order. We can experiment, try many different jobs, have many different relationships and adventures. Commitments to a single career or person feel like unnecessary restrictions on this freedom.

Some of us, however, react the opposite way: Frightened of the chaos, we quickly opt for a career that is practical and lucrative, hopefully related to some of our interests, but not necessarily. What motivates us is to somehow establish the stability that is so hard to find in this world.

Both paths, however, tend to lead to some problems further down the road. In the first case, trying so many things out, we never really develop solid skills in one particular area. Because of this our career possibilities begin to narrow. Although we might not like to admit it to ourselves, our freedom can begin to wear on us.

In the second case, the career we committed to in our twenties might begin to feel a bit lifeless in our thirties. We chose it for practical purposes, and it has little connection to what actually interests us in life. Perhaps we need some new, exciting career or relationship or adventure.

In either case, we do what we can to manage our frustrations. But as the years go by, we start to experience bouts of pain that we cannot deny or repress.

This pain comes in several forms.

We feel increasingly *bored*. Not really engaged in our work, we turn to various distractions to occupy our restless minds. But by the law of diminishing returns, we need to continually find new and stronger forms of diversion. Only when we are alone or in down moments do we actually experience the chronic boredom that motivates many of our actions and eats away at us.

We feel increasingly *insecure*. We all have dreams and a sense of our own potential. If we have wandered aimlessly through life or gone astray, we begin to become aware of the discrepancy between our dreams and reality. We have no solid accomplishments.

We often feel *anxious* and *stressed* but are never quite certain as to why. We steered clear of tough choices and stressful situations. But then they crop up in the present—we are forced to finish something by a deadline, or we suddenly become ambitious and want to realize a dream of ours. We have not learned in the past how to handle such situations, and the anxiety and stress overwhelm us. Our avoidance leads to a low-grade, continual anxiety.

And finally, we feel *depressed*. All of us want to believe that there is some purpose and meaning to our life, that we are connected to something larger than ourselves. Without that conviction, we experience an emptiness and depression that we will ascribe to other factors.

By our nature we humans crave a sense of direction. But the human mind is a bottomless pit—it provides us with endless mental spaces to explore. At any moment, we could choose to go in a hundred different directions. Without belief systems or conventions in place, we seem to have no obvious compass points to guide our behavior and decisions, and this can be maddening.

Fortunately there is one way out of this predicament, and it is by nature available to each and every one of us. There is no need to look for gurus or to grow nostalgic for the past and its certainties. A compass and guidance system does exist. It comes from looking for and discovering the *individual* purpose to our lives. It is the path taken by the greatest achievers and contributors to the advancement of human culture, and we only have to see the path to take it. Here's how it works.

Each human individual is radically unique. This uniqueness is inscribed in us in three ways—the one-of-a-kind configuration of our DNA, the particular way our brains are wired, and our experiences as we go through life, experiences that are unlike any other's. Consider this uniqueness as a seed that is planted at birth, with potential growth. And this uniqueness has a purpose.

Striving to connect to and cultivate this uniqueness provides us a path to follow, an internal guidance system through life. But connecting to this system does not come easily. Normally the signs of our uniqueness are clearer to us in early childhood. We found ourselves naturally drawn to particular subjects or activities, despite the influence of our parents. We can call these *primal inclinations*. They speak to us, like a voice. But as we get older, that voice becomes drowned out by parents, peers, teachers, the culture at large.

To tap into the guidance system, we must make the connection to our uniqueness as strong as possible, and learn to trust that voice.

When we engage this internal guidance system, all of the negative emotions that plague us in our aimlessness are neutralized and even turned around into positive ones. For instance, we may feel *boredom* in the process of accumulating skills. Practice can be tedious. But we can embrace the tedium, knowing of the tremendous benefits to come.

With a sense of purpose, we feel much less *insecure*. We have an overall sense that we are advancing, realizing some or all of our potential. We can begin to look back at various accomplishments, small or large. We know who we are, and this self-awareness becomes our anchor in life.

With this guidance system in place, we can turn *anxiety* and *stress* into productive emotions. In trying to reach our goals—a book, a business, winning a political campaign—we have to manage a great deal of anxiety and uncertainty, making daily decisions on what to do. We develop the ability to regulate our anxiety—enough to keep us going and keep improving the work, but not so much as to paralyze us.

And finally, with a sense of purpose we are less prone to *depression*. Yes, low moments are inevitable. But more often we feel excited and lifted above the pettiness that so often marks daily life in the modern world.

Your task as a student of human nature is twofold: First, you must become aware of the primary role that a sense of purpose plays in human life. Look at the people around you and gauge what is guiding their behavior, seeing patterns in their choices. Are they mostly after pleasure, money, attention, power for its own sake, or a cause to join? These are what we shall call *false purposes*, and they lead to obsessive behavior and various dead ends. Once you identify people as motivated by a false purpose, you should avoid hiring or working with them, as they will tend to draw you downward with their unproductive energy.

You will also notice some people who are struggling to find their purpose in the form of their calling in life. Perhaps you can help them or you can help each other. And finally, you may recognize a few people who have a relatively high sense of purpose. They will draw you upward.

Your second task is to find *your* sense of purpose and elevate it by making the connection to it as deep as possible. If you are young, use what you find to give an overall framework to your restless energy. Explore the world freely, accumulate adventures, but all within a certain framework. Most important, accumulate skills. If you are older and have gone astray, take the skills you have acquired and find ways to gently channel them in the direction that will eventually mesh with your inclinations and spirit. Avoid sudden and drastic career changes that are impractical.

In any event, you will want to go as far as you can in cultivating your uniqueness and the originality that goes with it. You are one of a kind. That represents true freedom and the ultimate power we humans can possess.

Strategies for Developing a High Sense of Purpose

Once you commit yourself to developing or strengthening your sense of purpose, then the hard work begins. You will face many enemies and obstacles impeding your progress—the distracting voices of others who instill doubts about your calling and your uniqueness; your own boredom and frustrations with the work itself and your slow progress; the lack of trustworthy criticism from people to help you; the levels of anxiety you must manage; and finally, the burnout that often accompanies focused labor over long periods. The following five strategies are designed to help you move past these obstacles. They are in a loose order, the first being the essential starting point. You will want to put them all into practice to ensure continual movement forward.

Discover your calling in life. You begin this strategy by looking for signs of primal inclinations in your earliest years, when they were often the clearest. What you are looking for is moments in which you were unusually fascinated by a particular subject, or certain objects, or specific activities and forms of play.

These moments of visceral attraction occurred suddenly and without any prodding from parents or friends. It would be hard to put into words why they occurred; they are signs of something beyond our personal control.

Examine moments in your life when certain tasks or activities felt natural and easy to you, similar to swimming with a current. In performing such activities, you have a greater tolerance for the tedium of practicing. People's criticisms don't discourage you so easily; you want to learn. You can contrast this with other subjects or tasks that you find deeply boring and unfulfilling, which frustrate you.

Related to this, you will want to figure out the particular form of intelligence that your brain is wired for. This could be mathematics and logic, physical activity, words, images, or music. We could also add to this social intelligence, a superior sensitivity to people. When you are engaged in the activity that feels right, it will correspond to that form of intelligence for which your brain is most suited.

From these various factors you should be able to spot the outline of your calling. In essence, in going through this process you are discovering yourself, what makes you different, what predates the opinions of others.

If you are young and just starting out in your career, you will want to explore a relatively wide field related to your inclinations. If you are older and have more experience, you will want to take the skills you have already developed and find a way to adapt them more in the direction of your true calling. Remember that the calling could be combining several fields that fascinate you.

Use resistance and negative spurs. The key to success in any field is first developing skills in various areas, which you can later combine in unique and creative ways. But the process of doing so can be tedious and painful, as you become aware of your limitations and relative lack of skill. Most people, consciously or unconsciously, seek to avoid tedium, pain, and any form of adversity. You must choose to move in the opposite direction. You want to embrace negative experiences, limitations, and even pain as the perfect means of building up your skill levels and sharpening your sense of purpose.

As you progress on your path, you will be subject to more and more of people's criticisms. Some of them might be constructive and worth paying attention to, but many of them come from envy. You can recognize the latter by the person's emotional tone in expressing their negative opinions. They go a little too far, speak with a bit too much vehemence; they make it personal, instilling doubts about your overall ability, emphasizing your personality more than the work; they lack specific details about what and how to improve. Once recognized, the trick is not to internalize these criticisms in any form. Instead, use their negative opinions to motivate you and add to your sense of purpose.

Absorb purposeful energy. We humans are extremely susceptible to the moods and energy of other people. For this reason, you want to avoid too much contact with those who have a low or false sense of purpose. On the other hand, you always want to try to find and associate with those who have a high sense of purpose. This could be the perfect mentor or teacher or partner on a project. Such people will tend to bring out the best in you, and you will find it easier and even refreshing to receive their criticisms.

You want to find people who are pragmatic and not merely those who are charismatic or visionaries. If possible, collect around you a group of people from different fields, as friends or associates, who have similar energy. You will help elevate one another's sense of purpose. Do not settle for virtual associations or mentors.

Create a ladder of descending goals. Operating with long-term goals will bring you tremendous clarity and resolve. The problem, however, is that they will also tend to generate anxiety as you look at all you have to do to reach them from the present vantage point.

To manage such anxiety, you must create a ladder of smaller goals along the way, reaching down to the present. Such objectives are simpler the further down the ladder you go, and you can realize them in relatively short time frames, giving you moments of satisfaction and a sense of progress.

Remember that what you are after is a series of practical results and accomplishments, not a list of unrealized dreams and aborted projects.

Lose yourself in the work. Perhaps the greatest difficulty you will face in maintaining a high and consistent sense of purpose is the level of commitment that is required over time and the sacrifices that go with this. You have to handle many moments of frustration, boredom, and failure, and the endless temptations in our culture for more immediate pleasures. And as the years pile up, you can face burnout.

To offset this tedium, you need to have moments of flow in which your mind becomes so deeply immersed in the work that you are transported beyond your ego.

These experiences cannot be manufactured, but you can set the stage for them and vastly increase your odds. First, it is essential to wait until you are further along in the process—at least more than halfway through a project, or after several years of study in your field.

Second, you must plan on giving yourself uninterrupted time with the work—as many hours in the day as possible, and as many days in the week. For this purpose, you have to rigorously eliminate the usual level of distractions, even plan on disappearing for a period of time.

Third, the emphasis must be on the work, never on yourself or the desire for recognition. You are fusing your mind with the work itself, and any intrusive thoughts from your ego or doubts about yourself or personal obsessions will interrupt the flow.

The Lure of False Purposes

The gravitational pull we feel toward finding a purpose comes from two elements in human nature. First, unable to rely on instincts as other animals do, we require some means of having a sense of direction, a way to guide and restrict our behavior. Second, we humans are aware of our puniness as individuals in a world with billions of others in a vast universe. We need to feel larger than just the individuals we are, and connected to something that transcends us.

Human nature being what it is, however, many people seek to create purpose and a feeling of transcendence on the cheap, to find it in the easiest and most accessible way, with the least amount of effort. Such people give themselves over to *false purposes*, those that merely supply the illusion of purpose and transcendence. We can contrast them with real purposes in the following way: The real purpose comes from within. It is an idea, a calling, a sense of mission that we feel personally and intimately connected to. False purposes come from external sources—belief systems that we swallow whole, conformity to what other people are doing.

Here are five of the most common forms of false purposes that have appealed to humans since the beginning of civilization.

The pursuit of pleasure: For many of us, work is just an irritating necessity of life. What really motivates us is avoiding pain, and finding as much pleasure as possible in our time outside work. The pleasures we pursue can take various forms—sex, stimulants, entertainment, games of all sorts.

No matter the objects of the pursuit, they tend to lead to a dynamic of diminishing returns. The moments of pleasure we get tend to get duller through repetition. We need either more and more of the same or constantly new diversions.

This form of false purpose is very common in the world today, largely because of the cornucopia of distractions we can choose from. But it goes against a basic element of human nature: to have deeper levels of pleasure, we have to learn to limit ourselves.

All of us require pleasurable moments outside work, ways to relieve our tension. But when we operate with a sense of purpose, we know the value of limiting ourselves, opting for depth of experience rather than overstimulation.

Causes and cults: People have a profound need to believe in something, and in the absence of great unifying belief systems, this void is easily filled by all kinds of microcauses and cults.

We can recognize a microcause or cult by the vagueness of what its disciples want, which is a clear sign that their group is merely about the release of emotions.

Allying ourselves with a cause can be an important part of our sense of purpose. But it must emerge from an internal process in which we have thought deeply about the subject and are committing ourselves to the cause as part of our life's work.

Money and success: For many people, the pursuit of money and status can supply them with plenty of motivation and focus. Such types would consider figuring out their calling in life a monumental waste of time and an antiquated notion. But in the long run this philosophy often yields the most impractical of results.

First, more often than not such types enter the field in which they can make the most money the fastest. Often they make big mistakes in their obsessive pursuit of money because their thinking is so short term.

Second, money and success that last come from remaining original and not mindlessly following the path that others are following. If we make money our primary goal, we never truly cultivate our uniqueness, and eventually someone younger and hungrier will supplant us.

And finally, what often motivates people in this quest is to simply have more money and status than other people, and to feel superior. With that standard, it is difficult to know when they have enough, because there are always people with more.

Many of the most successful, famous, and wealthy individuals do not begin with an obsession with money and status. Concentrate on maintaining a high sense of purpose, and the success will flow to you naturally.

Attention: People have always pursued fame and attention as a way to feel enlarged and more important. But this false sense of purpose has become greatly democratized and widespread through social media. Now almost any one of us can have the quantity of attention that past kings and conquerors could only dream about. Our self-image and self-esteem become tied to the attention we receive on a daily basis.

As with money and success, we have a much greater chance of attracting attention by developing a high sense of purpose and creating work that will naturally draw people to it. When the attention is unexpected, as with the success we suddenly have, it is all the more pleasurable.

Cynicism: According to Friedrich Nietzsche, "Man would rather have the void as purpose than be void of purpose." Cynicism, the feeling that there is no purpose or meaning in life, is what we shall call having "the void as purpose." In the world today, with growing disenchantment with politics and the belief systems of the past, this form of the false purpose is becoming increasingly common.

As hunters for purpose and meaning, we want to move in the opposite direction. Reality is not brutal and ugly—it contains much that is sublime, beautiful, and worthy of wonder. We see this in the great works of other achievers. We want to have more encounters with the Sublime. We see a purpose behind everything that we experience and see. In the end, what we want is to fuse the curiosity and excitement we had toward the world as children, when almost everything seemed enchanting, with our adult intelligence.

> The whole law of human existence consists in nothing other than a man's always being able to bow before the immeasurably great. If people are deprived of the immeasurably great, they will not live and will die in despair. The immeasurable and infinite are as necessary for man as the small planet he inhabits.
>
> *—Fyodor Dostoyevsky*

14

Resist the Downward Pull of the Group

◇

The Law of Conformity

We have a side to our character that we are generally unaware of—our social personality, the different person we become when we operate in groups of people. In the group setting, we unconsciously imitate what others are saying and doing. We think differently, more concerned with fitting in and believing what others believe. We feel different emotions, infected by the group mood. We are more prone to taking risks, to acting irrationally, because everyone else is. This social personality can come to dominate who we are. Listening so much to others and conforming our behavior to them, we slowly lose a sense of our uniqueness and the ability to think for ourselves. The only solution is to develop self-awareness and a superior understanding of the changes that occur in us in groups. With such intelligence, we can become superior social actors, able to outwardly fit in and cooperate with others on a high level, while retaining our independence and rationality.

> When people are free to do as they please, they usually imitate each other.
>
> *—Eric Hoffer*

Keys to Human Nature

At certain moments in life, we humans may experience an energy that is powerful, with sensations unlike any other, but this energy is something we rarely discuss or analyze. We can describe it as an intense feeling of belonging to a group, and we often experience it in the following situations.

Let us say we find ourselves in a large audience for a concert, sporting event, or political rally. At a certain point, waves of excitement, anger, or joy move through us, shared by thousands of others. In a similar vein, perhaps we have to give a talk before a group. If we are not too nervous and the crowd is on our side, we experience a swelling of emotion from deep within. Or perhaps we find ourselves working in a group with a critical goal to reach within a short time frame. We feel a charge of energy that comes from feeling connected to others who are working with the same urgent spirit.

The above feelings are not registered rationally; they come to us in automatic bodily sensations—goose bumps, racing heartbeat, extra vitality and power. Let us call us this energy the *social force*, a type of invisible force field that affects and binds a group of people through shared sensations and creates an intense feeling of connection.

We can observe several interesting elements to the social force: First, *it exists inside us and outside us at the same time*. When we experience the bodily sensations mentioned above, we are almost certain that others on our side are feeling the same.

We can also say *this force differs, depending on the size and chemistry of the particular group*. In general, the larger the group, the more intense is the effect. When we are among a very large group of people who seem to share our ideas or values, we feel quite a rush of increased strength and vitality, as well as communal warmth or heat that comes from feeling that we belong.

And finally, *we are drawn to this force*. We feel attracted to numbers—a stadium full of partisan supporters of a team, choirs of people singing, parades, carnivals, concerts, religious assemblies, and political conventions.

The social force is neither positive nor negative. It is simply a physiological part of our nature. In general, to the degree that the social force tends to degrade our ability to think independently and rationally, we can say it exerts a downward pull into more primitive ways of behaving, unsuited to modern conditions.

The social force, however, can be used and shaped for *positive* purposes, for high-level cooperation and empathy, for an upward pull, which we experience when we create something together in a group.

What we need more than anything is *group intelligence*. This intelligence includes a thorough understanding of the effect that groups have on our thinking and emotions; with such awareness, we can resist the downward pull.

To acquire this intelligence, we must study and master two aspects of the social force—the individual effect of groups on us and the patterns and dynamics that groups will almost always tend to fall into.

The Individual Effect

The desire to fit in: *The first and primary effect on you in any group is the desire to fit in and cement your sense of belonging.*

The first way you do this is through appearances. You dress and present yourself more or less as the others do in the group.

The second and more important way you fit in is by adopting the ideas, beliefs, and values of the group. The longer you are in the group, the stronger and more insidious this effect.

In the long run, it is much better to confront your conformity to the group ethos, so that you can become aware of it as it happens and control the process to some degree.

The need to perform: Stemming from this first effect is the second effect—*in the group setting, we are always performing.* It is not just that we conform in appearances and thinking but that we exaggerate our agreement and *show* others that we belong. In the group, we become actors, molding what we say and do so that others accept and like us and see us as loyal team members.

As part of this performance, we minimize our flaws and display what we consider our strengths. You should feel no shame about this need; better to be aware, to retain that inner distance, and to transform yourself into a conscious and superior actor, capable of altering your expression to fit the subgroup and impressing people with your positive qualities.

Emotional contagion: Like all social animals, we are primed from an early age to sense and pick up the emotions of others, particularly those close to us. This is the third effect of the group on us—*the contagiousness of emotions.*

You can observe this in yourself by looking at your own emotions in the moment and trying to decipher the effect others might have had on them. Discern which emotions are the most contagious for you and how your emotions shift with the various groups and subgroups you pass through. Awareness of this gives you the power to control it.

Hypercertainty: When we are in the group, we feel the urgency to act. We feel the pressure to decide and get behind the decision. And so the fourth effect on us is *to make us feel more certain about what we and our colleagues are doing, which makes us all the more prone to taking risks.*

Whenever you feel unusually certain and excited about a plan or idea, you must step back and gauge whether it is a viral group effect operating on you. Never relinquish your ability to doubt, reflect, and consider other options—your rationality as an individual is your only protection against the madness that can overcome a group.

Group Dynamics

Since the beginning of recorded history, we can observe certain patterns that human groups fall into almost automatically, as if they were subject to particular mathematical or physical laws. The following are the most common dynamics that you must study in the groups that you belong to or pass through.

Group culture: The group will always have some type of identifiable culture and spirit. Two things to keep in mind: First, the culture will often center on an ideal that the group imagines for itself—liberal, modern, progressive, ruthlessly competitive, tasteful, et cetera. Second, this culture will often reflect the founders of the group, particularly if they have a strong personality.

Group rules and codes: For any human group, disorder and anarchy are too distressing. And so standards of conduct and rules for how to do things quickly evolve and become set. These rules and codes are never written down but are implicit. When you are new to a group, you must pay extra attention to these tacit codes. Look at who's rising and who's falling within the group—signs of the standards that govern success and failure.

The group court: Observe any community of chimpanzees at the zoo, and you will notice the existence of an alpha male and other chimpanzees adapting their behavior to him, fawning, imitating, and struggling to forge closer ties. This is the prehuman version of the court. The courtiers may look different now, but their behavior and strategies are pretty much the same. You must take note of a few of these behavioral patterns. See more on this below.

First, courtiers have to gain the attention of leaders and ingratiate themselves in some way. The most immediate way to do this is through flattery. Second, you must pay great attention to the other courtiers. Learn to downplay your successes, to listen (or seem to listen) deeply to the ideas of others, strategically giving them credit and praise in meetings, paying attention to *their* insecurities. Third, you need to be aware of the types of courtiers you will find in most courts and the particular dangers they can pose.

Keep in mind that there is no way to opt out of the court dynamic. Better to be the consummate courtier and find some pleasure in the game of court strategy.

The group enemy: Look at the group you belong to, and you will inevitably see some sort of enemy or bogeyman to push against. What you require is the ability to detach yourself from this dynamic and to see the "enemy" as it is, minus the distortions. Take this even a step further by learning from the enemy, adapting some of its superior strategies.

Group factions: Over enough time, individuals in a group will begin to split off into factions. If left alone, factions can become so powerful they take over and depose or control the leaders themselves. Better to tighten the whole group by creating a positive culture that excites and unifies its members, making factions less attractive.

Your task as a student of human nature is twofold: First, you must become a consummate observer of yourself as you interact with groups of any size. Begin with the assumption that you are not nearly as much of an individual as you imagine. We are all permeable to the influence of the group. What makes us more permeable is our insecurities. Your goal must be to lower your permeability by raising your self-esteem.

Your second task is to become a consummate observer of the groups you belong to or interact with. Consider yourself an anthropologist studying the strange customs of an alien tribe. You are catching the social force as it molds the group into an organism, the sum greater than its parts. Your goal in this second task is to maintain as tight a grip on reality as possible. Your strategies and decisions will be all the more effective for this.

Just as groups tend to exert a downward pull on our emotions and behavior, we can also experience or imagine the opposite—a group that exerts an upward pull. We shall call this ideal the *reality group* (see more on this below). It consists of members who feel free to contribute their diverse opinions, whose minds are open, and whose focus is on getting work done and cooperating on a high level. By maintaining your individual spirit and your grip on reality, you will help create or enrich this ideal team of people.

The Court and Its Courtiers

Courtiers tend to fall into certain types, depending on deep patterns stemming from childhood. The following are seven of the more common types you will find.

The Intriguer: These individuals can be particularly difficult to recognize. They seem intensely loyal to the boss and to the group. But this is a mask they wear; behind the scenes they are continually intriguing to amass more power. They generally have a disdain for the boss that they are careful to conceal.

In identifying this type, you must look behind the efficient and loyal front and even the charm. Keep your eye instead on their maneuvers and their impatience to rise from within. Realize that when they are looking at you, they are thinking of how they can use you as a tool or stepping-stone. It is best to keep your distance and not become one of their pawns, nor their enemy.

The Stirrer: This type is generally riddled with insecurities but adept at disguising them from those in the court. They feel deep wells of resentment and envy for what others seem to have that they don't. Their game is to infect the group with doubts and anxieties, stirring up trouble, which puts them at the center of action and may allow them to get closer to the leader.

If you feel the group succumbing to viral anxiety about some vague threat, try to locate the source of this—you might have a Stirrer in your midst. When dealing with a known Stirrer, do not directly or indirectly insult or show disrespect.

The Gatekeeper: The goal of the game for these types is gaining exclusive access to leaders, monopolizing the flow of information to them. They often rise to their position by fawning over the genius and perfection of the leader, whom they idealize. In gaining such proximity, they also get to see the leaders' dark sides and learn of their weaknesses; this unconsciously binds leaders even more tightly to Gatekeepers, whom they might fear alienating. Having such power over the admired leader is their endgame.

Once such types are installed in power, they are extremely dangerous—running afoul of them in any way will cut off key access to the one player on the board who matters the most, and other perks. Recognize them early on by their shameless sycophancy toward the boss. In general, it is best to recognize their power and remain on their good side.

The Shadow Enabler: More than others, leaders

have to keep their Shadow side under wraps. Unconsciously their Shadow is yearning to come out. In steps the Enabler, one of the cleverest and most diabolical courtiers of all.

These types are the masters at detecting repressed desires in others, including leaders. Having established contact with the leader's Shadow, the Enabler then takes this further, with suggestions of possible actions for leaders, ways to vent their frustrations, with the Enabler handling it all and serving as protection.

It is too dangerous to cross such types, unless what they are planning is so dark that it is worth risking your own position to stop them. Take heart that their careers are generally short. Maintain a polite distance.

The Court Jester: Almost every court has its Jester. They can be the court cynic and scoffer, who has license to poke fun at almost everyone and everything, including sometimes the leaders themselves, who tolerate this because it shows their apparent lack of insecurity and sense of humor. These types fall into such roles because secretly they have a fear of responsibility and a dread of failing. They know that as Jesters they are not taken seriously and are given little actual power.

Never take their existence as a sign that you can freely imitate their behavior. There is rarely more than one Jester per court for a reason. Better to reserve your nonconformity for your private life, or until you have amassed more power.

The Mirrorer: These types are often among the most successful courtiers of all, because they are capable of playing the double game to the hilt—they are adept at charming leaders *and* fellow courtiers, maintaining a broad base of support. They are masters at reflecting back to people their own moods and ideas, making them feel validated without sensing the manipulation, as opposed to using overt flattery.

This is a role you might want to consider playing in the court because of the power it brings, but to pull it off you will have to be a great reader of people, sensitive to their nonverbal cues. You want to be able to mirror their moods, not just their ideas. With leaders, you must be aware of their idealized opinion of themselves and always confirm it in some way, or even encourage them to live up to it.

The Favorite and the Punching Bag: These two types occupy the highest and lowest rungs of the court. Every king or queen must have his or her Favorite within the court. As opposed to the other types, whose power generally depends on efficiency and demonstrations of abject loyalty, the Favorite's rise in power is often based on cultivating a more personal, friend-like relationship.

Try to avoid being lured into taking this position. Make your power dependent on your accomplishments and your usefulness, not on the friendly feelings people have for you.

Much as in any children's playground, in the court there is almost always a person who plays the role of the Punching Bag, whom everyone feels encouraged to laugh at in some way and feel superior to. Much of their ridicule will be behind the back of the targets, but they will sense it. Do not engage in this dynamic. Within the ruthless environment of the court, try to befriend the Punching Bag, showing a different way of behaving and taking the fun out of this cruel game.

The Reality Group

What creates a functional, healthy dynamic is the ability of the group to maintain a tight relationship to reality. The reality for a group is as follows: It exists in order to get things done, to make things, to solve problems. It has certain resources it can draw upon—the labor and strengths of its members, its finances. It operates in a particular environment that is almost always highly competitive and constantly changing. The healthy group puts primary emphasis on the work itself, on getting the most out of its resources and adapting to all of the inevitable changes. Not wasting time on endless political games, such a group can accomplish ten times more than the dysfunctional variety. It brings out the best in human nature—people's empathy, their ability to work with others on a high level. It remains the ideal for all of us. We shall call this ideal *the reality group*.

The following are five key strategies for achieving this, all of which should be put into practice.

Instill a collective sense of purpose. That social force that compels people to want to belong and to fit in you want to capture and channel for a higher purpose. You can accomplish this by establishing an ideal—your group has a definite purpose, a positive mission that unites its members. This purpose is not vague or implied but clearly stated and publicized.

To make this work, the group must practice what you preach. You want to establish a track record of results that reflect the group's ideal. You want to keep reminding the group of its mission, adapting it if necessary but never drifting from this core.

Assemble the right team of lieutenants. As the leader of a reality group, you need the ability to focus on the larger picture and the overall goals that matter. You have only so much mental energy and you must marshal it wisely. The greatest obstacle to this is your fear of delegating authority.

What you need to do from the outset is to cultivate a team of lieutenants, imbued with your spirit and the collective sense of purpose, whom you can trust to manage the execution of ideas. To achieve this, you must have the right standards—you do not base your selection on people's charm, and never hire friends. You want the most competent person for the job. You also give great consideration to their character.

You select for this team people who have skills that you lack, each individual with their particular strengths. They know their roles. You also want this team of lieutenants to be diverse in temperament, background, and ideas. Feeling a part of a team but able to bring their own creativity to the tasks will bring out the best in them, and this spirit will spread throughout the group.

Let information and ideas flow freely. Consider the open communication of ideas and information—about rivals, about what is happening on the streets or among your audience—the lifeblood of the group.

To achieve this, you want to encourage frank discussion up and down the line, with members trusting that they can do so. To allow for such openness, you must be careful in these discussions to not signal your own preference for a particular opinion or decision, as this will subtly tip the team into following your lead. Even bring in experts and outsiders to broaden the group's perspective.

Extend this open communication to the ability for the group to criticize itself and its performance, particularly after any mistakes or failures.

Infect the group with productive emotions. Infect the group with a sense of resolution that emanates from you. You are not upset by setbacks; you keep advancing and working on problems. The group sense this, and individuals feel embarrassed for becoming hysterical over the slightest shift in fortune. You can try to infect the group with confidence, but be careful that this does not slip into grandiosity. Your confidence and that of the group mostly stems from a successful track record.

Most important, showing a lack of fear and an overall openness to new ideas will have the most therapeutic effect of all. The members will become less defensive, which encourages them to think more on their own, and not operate as automatons.

Forge a battle-tested group. You want to be able to gauge the relative inner toughness of people before you are thrust into a crisis. Give various members some relatively challenging tasks or shorter deadlines than usual, and see how they respond. Some people rise to the occasion and even do better under stress; consider such people a treasure to hoard. Observe carefully how individuals react to the slight amount of chaos and uncertainty that unfold from this. Of course, in the aftermath of any crisis or failures, use such moments as a way to review people's inner strength or lack of it.

> Madness is something rare in individuals—but in groups, parties, peoples, and ages it is the rule.
>
> —*Friedrich Nietzsche*

15

Make Them Want to Follow You

—— ✧ ——

The Law of Fickleness

Although styles of leadership change with the times, one constant remains: people are always ambivalent about those in power. They want to be led but also to feel free; they want to be protected and enjoy prosperity without making sacrifices; they both worship the king and want to kill him. When you are the leader of a group, people are continually prepared to turn on you the moment you seem weak or experience a setback. Do not succumb to the prejudices of the times, imagining that what you need to do to gain their loyalty is to seem to be their equal or their friend; people will doubt your strength, become suspicious of your motives, and respond with hidden contempt. Authority is the delicate art of creating the appearance of power, legitimacy, and fairness while getting people to identify with you as a leader who is in their service. If you want to lead, you must master this art from early on in your life. Once you have gained people's trust, they will stand by you as their leader, no matter the bad circumstances.

That ... is the road to the obedience of compulsion.

But there is a shorter way to a nobler goal, the obedience of the will. When the interests of mankind are at stake, they will obey with joy the man whom they believe to be wiser than themselves. You may prove this on all sides: you may see how the sick man will beg the doctor to tell him what he ought to do, how a whole ship's company will listen to the pilot.

–Xenophon

Keys to Human Nature

We humans like to believe that the emotions we experience are simple and pure: we love certain people and hate others, we respect and admire this individual and have nothing but disdain for another. The truth is that this is almost never the case. *It is a fundamental fact of human nature that our emotions are almost always ambivalent, rarely pure and simple.* We can feel love and hostility at the same time, or admiration and envy.

Nowhere is this fundamental aspect of human nature more evident than in our relationship toward leaders. This ambivalence toward leaders operates in the following way.

On the one hand, we intuitively recognize the need for leaders. In any group, people have their narrow agendas and competing interests. Without leaders who stand above these competing interests and who see the larger picture, the group would be in trouble. Therefore, we crave leadership and unconsciously feel disoriented, even hysterical, without someone fulfilling this role.

On the other hand, we also tend to fear and even despise those who are above us. This essential ambivalence tips toward the negative when leaders show signs of abuse, insensitivity, or incompetence. No matter how powerful the leaders, no matter how much we might admire them, below the surface sits this ambivalence, and it makes people's loyalties notoriously fickle and volatile.

Those in power will tend to notice only the smiles of their employees and the applause they receive at meetings, and they will mistake such support for reality. They do not realize that people almost always show such deference to those above them, because their personal fate is in the hands of such leaders and they cannot afford to show their true feelings. And so leaders are rarely aware of the underlying ambivalence that is there even when things are going well. If leaders make some mistakes, or if their power seems shaky, suddenly they will see the mistrust and loss of respect that had been invisibly building up, as the members of the group or the public turn on them with an intensity that is surprising and shocking. Look at the news to see how quickly leaders in any field can lose support and respect, and how quickly they are judged by their latest success or failure.

To the ancient Romans, those who had founded their republic possessed tremendous wisdom. Their ancestors had demonstrated this wisdom by how strong and long-lasting were the institutions they had established, and how they had transformed their provincial town into the preeminent power in the known world. To the extent that Roman senators and leaders returned to this basic wisdom and embodied the ideals of the founders, they had *authority*—an augmented presence, an increased prestige and credibility. Such leaders did not have to resort to speeches or to force. Roman citizens willingly followed their lead and accepted their ideas or advice. Their every word and deed seemed to carry extra weight. This gave them greater leeway in making hard decisions; they were not judged merely by their latest success.

Having leaders who exuded authority was a way to get things done and maintain a degree of unity. And it required that such leaders embody the highest of ideals, ones that transcended the pettiness of daily political life.

This Roman model, which represents an adherence to a higher purpose, remains the essential ingredient for all true forms of authority. And this is how we must operate if we wish to establish such authority in the world today.

First and foremost, we must understand the fundamental task of any leader—to provide a far-reaching vision, to see the global picture, to work for the greater good of the group and maintain its unity. Focusing on the future and the larger picture should consume much of our thinking.

At the same time, however, we must see leadership as a dynamic relationship we have with those being led. We need to attune ourselves to the shifting moods of the members of the group. We must never assume we have their support. Our empathy must be visceral—we can *feel* when members are losing respect for us. As part of the dynamic, we need to realize that when we show our respect and trust toward those below us, such feelings will flow back to us.

When leaders fail to establish these twin pillars of authority—vision and empathy—what often happens is the following: Those in the group feel the disconnect and distance between them and leadership. They know that deep down they are viewed as replaceable pawns. And so, in subtle ways, they begin to feel resentful and to lose respect. They listen less attentively to what such leaders say. They spend more hours in the day thinking of their own interests and future. They join or form factions. They work at half or three-quarter speed.

On the other hand, if we intuitively or consciously follow the path of establishing authority, as described above, we have a much different effect on the group dynamic. The ambivalence of the members or the public does not go away—that would violate human nature—but it becomes manageable. People will still waver and have moments of doubt or envy, but they will more quickly forgive us for any mistakes and move past their suspicions. We have established enough trust for that to happen.

It is always within our capacity to reach this ideal, and if the members lose respect and trust in us, we must see this as our fault.

Your task as a student of human nature is threefold: First

you must make yourself a consummate observer of the phenomenon of authority, using as a measuring device the degree of influence people wield without the use of force or motivational speeches. You begin this process by looking at your own family and gauging which parent, if any, exercised greater authority over you and your siblings. You look at the teachers and mentors in your life, some of whom distinguished themselves by the powerful effect they had on you. Their words and the example they set still reverberate in your mind. You observe your own bosses in action, looking at their effect not only on you and other individuals but also on the group as a whole. Lastly, you look at the various leaders in the news. In all these cases, you want to determine the source of their authority or lack of it.

Second, you want to develop some of the habits and strategies that will serve you well in projecting authority.

As part of this process, you need to reflect on the effect you have on people: Are you constantly arguing, trying to impose your will, finding much more resistance than you expect to your ideas and projects? If you are just starting out, sometimes this cannot be helped—people generally don't respect the ideas of those lower down in the hierarchy. But sometimes it could stem from your own actions, as you violate many of the principles described above.

Do not take people's smiles and expression of assent for reality. In general, you want to heighten your sensitivity to others, looking in particular at those moments when you can *feel* people's disrespect, or your authority on the wane.

Third and most important, you must not fall for the counterproductive prejudices of the times we live in, in which the very concept of authority is often misunderstood and despised. Today we confuse authority with leaders in general, and since so many of them in the world seem more interested in preserving their power and enriching themselves, naturally we have doubts about the very concept itself. We also live in fiercely democratic times. "Why should we ever have to follow a person of authority, and assume such an inferior role?" we might ask ourselves.

As students of human nature, we must recognize the myriad dangers of our prejudice against authority figures. To acknowledge people of authority in the world is not an admission of our own inferiority but rather an acceptance of human nature and the need for such figures. People of authority should not be seen as self-serving or tyrannical—in fact, those are the qualities that diminish their authority. They are not relics of the past but people who fulfill a necessary function and whose style adapts with the times. Authority can be an eminently democratic phenomenon.

Strategies for Establishing Authority

Remember that the essence of authority is that people willingly follow your lead. They chose to adhere to your words and advice. They want your wisdom. Certainly at times you may have to use force, rewards and punishments, and inspiring speeches. It is only a matter of degree. The less your need of such devices, the greater your authority. And so you must think of continually striving to engage people's willpower and overcome their natural resistances and ambivalence. That is what the following strategies are designed to do. Put them all into practice.

Find your authority style: Authenticity. The authority you establish must emerge naturally from your character, from the particular strengths you possess. Think of certain archetypes of authority: one of them suits you best. A notable archetype is the *Deliverer*, such as Moses or Martin Luther King Jr., an individual determined to deliver people from evil.

Another archetype would be the *Founder*. These are the ones who establish a new order in politics or business. They generally have a keen sense of trends and a great aversion to the status quo. Related to this archetype would be the *Visionary Artist*, such as Pablo Picasso or the jazz artist John Coltrane or the film director David Lynch. These artists learn the conventions in their field and then turn them upside down.

Other archetypes could include the *Truth Seeker* (people who have no tolerance for lies and politicking); the *Quiet Pragmatist* (they want nothing more than to fix things that are broken, and have infinite patience); the *Healer* (they have a knack for finding what will fulfill and unify people); the *Teacher* (they have a way of getting people to initiate action and learn from their mistakes). You must identify with one of these archetypes, or any others that are noticeable in culture.

By bringing out a style that is natural to you, you give the impression that it is something beyond you, as if your sense of justice or nose for trends came from your DNA or were a gift from the gods.

Focus outwardly: the Attitude. We humans are self-absorbed by nature and spend most of our time focusing inwardly on our emotions, on our wounds, on our fantasies. You want to develop the habit of reversing this as much as possible. You do this in three ways. First, you hone your listening skills, absorbing yourself in the words and nonverbal cues of others. You do not take people's smiles and approving looks for reality but rather sense the underlying tension or fascination.

Second, you dedicate yourself to earning people's respect. You earn their respect by respecting their individual needs and by proving that you are working for the greater good. Third, you consider being a leader a tremendous responsibility, the welfare of the group hanging on your every decision. You feel a deep and visceral connection to the group, seeing your fate and theirs as deeply intertwined.

If you exude this attitude, people will feel it, and it will open them up to your influence.

Cultivate the third eye: the Vision. Most people

are locked in the moment. They are prone to overreacting and panicking, to seeing only a narrow part of the reality facing the group. Those who maintain their presence of mind and elevate their perspective above the moment tap into the visionary powers of the human mind and cultivate that third eye for unseen forces and trends. They stand out from the group, fulfill the true function of leadership, and create the aura of authority by seeming to possess the godlike ability to read the future. And this is a power that can be practiced and developed and applied to any situation.

As early in life as possible, you train yourself to disconnect from the emotions roiling the group. You force yourself to raise your vision, to imagine the larger picture. You entertain the perspective of the enemy; you listen to the ideas of outsiders; you open your mind to various possibilities. In this way, you gain a feel for the gestalt, or overall shape of the situation. You game out the possible trends, how things might play out in the future, and in particular how things could go wrong. You have infinite patience for this exercise. The more deeply you go into it, the more you can acquire the power to discern the future in some form.

Lead from the front: the Tone. As the leader, you must be seen working as hard as or even harder than everyone else. This sets the proper tone. The members will feel compelled to raise themselves up to your level to gain your approval. They will internalize your values and subtly imitate you.

It is important that you set this tone from the beginning. First impressions are critical. If you try later on to show you want to lead from the front, it will look forced and lack credibility. Equally important is to show some initial toughness; if people get the impression early on that they can maneuver you, they will do so mercilessly.

Begin this early on in your career by developing the highest possible standards for your own work and by training yourself to be constantly aware of how your manner and tone affect people in the subtlest of ways.

Stir conflicting emotions: the Aura. Most people are too predictable. To mix well in social situations, they assume a persona that is consistent—jovial, pleasing, bold, sensitive. They try to hide other qualities that they are afraid to show. As the leader, you want to be more mysterious, to establish a presence that fascinates people. By sending mixed signals, by showing qualities that are ever so slightly contrary, you cause people to pause in their instant categorizations and to think about who you really are. The more they think about you, the larger and more authoritative your presence.

Related to this, you must learn to balance presence and absence. If you are too present and familiar, always available and visible, you seem too banal. You give people no room to idealize you. But if you are too aloof, people cannot identify with you. In general, it is best to lean slightly more in the direction of absence, so that when you do appear before the group, you generate excitement and drama.

Never appear to take, always to give: the Taboo. Taking something from people they have assumed they possessed—money, rights or privileges, time that is their own—creates a basic insecurity and will call into question your authority and all the credit you have amassed. You make the members of the group feel uncertain about the future in a most visceral manner. Even the hint of this will harm your reputation. If sacrifices are necessary, you are the first to make them, and they are not simply symbolic. Try to frame any loss of resources or privileges as temporary, and make it clear how quickly you will restore them.

Related to this, you must avoid overpromising to people. In the moment, it might feel good to let them hear of the great things you will do for them, but people generally have an acute memory for promises, and if you fail to deliver, it will stick in their mind, even if you try to blame others or circumstances. If this happens a second time, your authority begins to sharply erode. Not giving what you promised to deliver will feel like something you have taken away. Everyone can talk a good game and promise, and so you seem like just anyone else we encounter, and the disappointment can be profound.

Rejuvenate your authority: Adaptability. Your authority will grow with each action that inspires trust and respect. But as you get older, the authority you established can become rigid and stodgy. You become the father figure who starts to seem oppressive by how long he has monopolized power, no matter how deeply people admired him in the past. A new generation inevitably emerges that is immune to your charm, to the aura you have created.

The first step in avoiding this danger is to maintain sensitivity, noting the moods behind people's words, gauging the effect you have on newcomers and young people. Losing that empathy should be your greatest fear, as you will begin to cocoon yourself in your great reputation.

The second step is to look for new markets and audiences to appeal to, which will force you to adapt. Without making a fool of yourself by attempting to appeal to a younger crowd that you cannot really understand, try to alter your style somewhat with the passing years. Such flexibility in those who are in their fifties and beyond will give you a touch of the divine and immortal—your spirit remains alive and open, and your authority is renewed.

The Inner Authority

We all have a higher and a lower self. At certain moments in life, we can definitely feel one part of the other as the stronger. When we accomplish things, when we finish what we start, we can sense the outlines of this higher self. But equally we know all too well the stirrings of the lower self, when we take everything personally and become petty, or when we want to escape reality through some addictive pleasure, or when we waste time, or when we feel confused and unmotivated.

Although we most often float between these two sides, if we look at ourselves closely, we have to admit that the lower half is the stronger one. It often takes great effort and awareness to tame this lower half and bring out the higher side; it is not our first impulse.

The key to making the struggle between the two sides more even and to perhaps tip the scales toward the higher is to cultivate what we shall call the *inner authority*. It serves as the voice, the conscience of our higher self. Think of this voice as dictating a code of behavior, and every day we must make ourselves listen to it. It tells us the following.

You have a responsibility to contribute to the culture and times you live in. Right now, you are living off the fruits of millions of people in the past who have made your life incomparably easier through their struggles and inventions. It is so easy to take this all for granted, to imagine that it all just came about naturally and that you are entitled to have all of these powers. That is the view of spoiled children, and you must see any signs of such an attitude within you as shameful. You are here not merely to gratify your impulses and consume what others have made but to make and contribute as well, to serve a higher purpose.

To serve this higher purpose, you must cultivate what is unique about you. Stop listening so much to the words and opinions of others, telling you who you are and what you should like and dislike. Judge things and people for yourself. Work every day on improving those skills that mesh with your unique spirit and purpose. Add to the needed diversity of culture by creating something that reflects your uniqueness.

In a world full of endless distractions, you must focus and prioritize. Certain activities are a waste of time. Certain people of a low nature will drag you down, and you must avoid them. Keep your eye on your long- and short-term goals, and remain concentrated and alert. Allow yourself the luxury of exploring and wandering creatively, but always with an underlying purpose.

You must adhere to the highest standards in your work. You strive for excellence, to make something that will resonate with the public and last. To maintain such standards, you must develop self-discipline and the proper work habits. You must pay great attention to the details in your work and place a premium value on effort. The first thought or idea that comes to you is most often incomplete and inadequate. Think more thoroughly and deeply about your ideas, some of which you must discard. Do not become attached to your initial ideas, but rather treat them roughly. Keep in mind that your life is short, that it could end any day. You must have a sense of urgency to make the most of this limited time. You don't need deadlines or people telling you what to do and when to finish. Any motivation you need comes from within. You are complete and self-reliant.

The select man, the excellent man is urged, by interior necessity, to appeal from himself to some standard beyond himself, superior to himself, whose service he freely accepts ... We distinguished the excellent man from the common man by saying that the former is one who makes great demands on himself, and the latter the one who makes no demands on himself, but contents himself with what he is, and is delighted with himself. Contrary to what is usually thought, it is the man of excellence ... who lives in essential servitude. Life has no savor for him unless he makes it consist in service to something transcendental. Hence he does not look upon the necessity of serving as an oppression. When, by chance, such necessity is lacking, he grows restless and invents some new standard, more difficult, more exigent, with which to coerce himself. This is life lived as a discipline—the noble life.

—*José Ortega y Gasset*

turn to love and channel it for creative ... oppress ... ... of ... secretly attacking problems ... ... other ... ... from great enterprises.

... are not gentle, friendly creatures wishing for ...
... ...
powerful urge for aggression that is often repressed ...
... ...

[Sigmund Freud]

16

See the Hostility Behind the Friendly Façade

—— ◇ ——

The Law of Aggression

On the surface, the people around you appear so polite and civilized. But beneath the mask, they are all inevitably dealing with frustrations. They have a need to influence people and gain power over circumstances. Feeling blocked in their endeavors, they often try to assert themselves in manipulative ways that catch you by surprise. And then there are those whose need for power and impatience to obtain it are greater than others. They turn particularly aggressive, getting their way by intimidating people, being relentless and willing to do almost anything. You must transform yourself into a superior observer of people's unsatisfied aggressive desires, paying extra attention to the chronic aggressors and passive aggressors in our midst. You must recognize the signs—the past patterns of behavior, the obsessive need to control everything in their environment—that indicate the dangerous types. They depend on making you emotional—afraid, angry—and unable to think straight. Do not give them this power. When it comes to your own aggressive energy, learn to tame and channel it for productive purposes—standing up for yourself, attacking problems with relentless energy, realizing great ambitions.

> Men are not gentle, friendly creatures wishing for love, who simply defend themselves if attacked ... A powerful desire for aggression has to be reckoned was part of their ... endowment.
>
> —Sigmund Freud

Keys to Human Nature

All of us understand that humans have been capable of much violence and aggression in the past and in the present. We know that out there in the world there are sinister criminals, greedy and unscrupulous businesspeople, belligerent negotiators, and sexual aggressors. But we create a sharp dividing line between those examples and us. We have a powerful block against imagining any kind of continuum or spectrum when it comes to our own aggressive moments and those of the more extreme variety in others. We in fact define the word to describe the stronger manifestations of aggression, excluding ourselves. It is always the other who is belligerent, who starts things, who is aggressive.

This is a profound misconception of human nature. Aggression is a tendency that is latent in every single human individual. It is a tendency wired into our species. We become the preeminent animal on this planet precisely because of our aggressive energy, supplemented by our intelligence and cunning. We cannot separate this aggressiveness from the way we attack problems, alter the environment to make our lives easier, fight injustice, or create anything on a large scale.

Aggression can serve positive purposes. At the same time, under certain circumstances, this energy can push us into antisocial behavior, into grabbing too much or pushing people around. These positive and negative aspects are two sides of the same coin. And although some individuals are clearly more aggressive than others, all of us are capable of slipping into that negative side. There is a continuum of human aggression, and we are all on the spectrum.

This energy cannot be denied or repressed; it will emerge in some way. But with awareness, we can begin to control and channel it for productive and positive purposes. To do so, we must understand the source of all human aggression, how it turns negative, and why some people become more aggressive than others.

The Source of Human Aggression

Unlike any other animal, we humans are aware of our mortality, and that we could die at any moment. Consciously and unconsciously this thought haunts us throughout our lives. We are aware that our position in life is never secure—we can lose our job, our social status, and our money, often for reasons beyond our control.

The people around us are equally unpredictable—we can never read their thoughts, anticipate their actions, or totally rely on their support. We are dependent on others, who often don't come through. We have certain innate desires for love, excitement, and stimulation, and it's often beyond our control to satisfy these desires in the way we would like. In addition, we all have certain insecurities that stem from wounds in our childhood. If events or people trigger these insecurities and reopen old wounds, we feel particularly vulnerable and weak.

With more chronically aggressive types, the sense of helplessness or frustration that we may feel upon occasion plagues them more deeply and more often. They feel chronically insecure and fragile and must cover this with an inordinate amount of power and control. Their need for power is too immediate and strong for them to accept the limits, and overrides any sense of compunction or social responsibility.

What this means is that human aggression stems from an underlying insecurity, as opposed to simply an impulse to hurt or take from others. Before any impulse to take aggressive action, aggressors are unconsciously processing feelings of helplessness and anxiety. They often perceive threats that are not really there, or exaggerate them. They take action to preempt the perceived attack of another or to grab for things in order to dominate a situation they feel may elude their control. When we look at any chronic aggressor around us, we must search for the underlying insecurity, the deep wound, the reverberating feelings of helplessness from their earliest years.

We must also be aware that aggressors see the people around them as objects to use. When they are listening to us, they are gauging the strength of our will and seeing how we can serve their purposes down the road. If they praise us or do us a favor, it is a way to further entrap and compromise us. We can see this in the nonverbal cues, in the eyes that look through us, in how thinly they are engaged in our stories. We must always try to make ourselves immune to any attempt at charm on their part, knowing what purpose it serves.

Your task as a student of human nature is threefold: First, you must stop denying the reality of your own aggressive tendencies. You are on the aggressive spectrum, like all of us. This assertive energy must be expended in some way and will tend to go in one of three directions.

First, we can channel this energy into our work, into patiently achieving things (*controlled aggression*). Second, we can channel it into *aggressive* or *passive-aggressive* behavior. Finally, we can turn it inward in the form of self-loathing, directing our anger and aggression at our own failings. You need to analyze how you handle your assertive energy. A way to judge yourself is to see how you handle moments of frustration and uncertainty, situations in which you have less control. Do you tend to lash out, grow angry and tense, and do things you later regret? Or do you internalize the anger and grow depressed?

You need to discipline and tame your natural

assertive energy. This is what we shall call *controlled aggression*, and it will lead to accomplishing great things.

Your second task is to make yourself a master observer of aggression in the people around you. When you look at your work world, for instance, imagine that you can visualize the continual war between people's different levels of will, and all of the intersecting arrows of such conflicts. If you stop focusing on people's words and the façade they present, and concentrate on their actions and their nonverbal cues, you can almost sense the level of aggressiveness they emanate.

Look for some telltale signs. First, if they have an unusually high number of enemies whom they have accumulated over the years, there must be a good reason, and not the one they tell you. Pay close attention to how they justify their actions in the world. Aggressors will tend to present themselves as crusaders, as some form of genius who cannot help the way they behave. They are creating great art, they say, or helping the little man. People who get in their way are infidels and evil. The louder and more extreme their narrative, the more you can be certain you are dealing with chronic aggressors. Focus on their actions, their past pattern of behavior, much more than anything they say.

Once you realize you are dealing with this type, you must use every ounce of your energy to disengage mentally, to gain control of your emotional response.

Finally, your third task as a student of human nature is to rid yourself of the denial of the very real aggressive tendencies in human nature itself and what such aggression might mean for our future as a species. This denial tends to take the form of one of two myths you are likely to believe in. The first myth is that long ago we humans were peace-loving creatures, in harmony with nature and our fellow humans. Recent finds in anthropology and archaeology, however, have proven beyond a shadow of a doubt that our ancestors (going back tens of thousands of years, well before civilization) engaged in warfare that was as murderous and brutal as anything in the present. They were hardly peaceful.

The other myth, more prevalent today, is that we may have been violent and aggressive in the past, but that we are currently evolving beyond this, becoming more tolerant, enlightened, and guided by our better angels. But the signs of human aggression are just as prevalent in our era as in the past. We can hold up as evidence the endless cycles of war, the acts of genocide, and the increasing hostility between states and ethnicities within states that continue well into this century. And our depredation of the environment has only gotten substantially worse, despite our awareness of the problem.

Passive Aggression—Its Strategies and How to Counter Them

Most of us are afraid of outright confrontation; we want to appear reasonably polite and sociable. But often it is impossible to get what we want without asserting ourselves in some way. And so all of us inevitably engage in behavior in which we assert ourselves indirectly, striving for control or influence as subtly as possible. Perhaps we take extra time to respond to people's communications, to signal a slight bit of disdain for them; or we seem to praise people but insert subtle digs that get under their skin and instill doubts.

We can call this form of aggression passive, in that we give the appearance that we are merely being ourselves, not *actively* manipulating or trying to influence people. Nevertheless, a message is sent that creates the effect we desire. In general, we must consider this everyday version of passive aggression to be merely an irritating part of social life, something we are all guilty of. We should be as tolerant as possible of this low-grade passive aggression that thrives in polite society.

Some people, however, are chronic passive aggressors. The following are the most common strategies employed by such aggressors, and ways to counter them.

The Subtle-Superiority Strategy: A friend, colleague, or employee is chronically late, but he or she always has a ready excuse that is logical, along with an apology that seems sincere. Or similarly, such individuals forget about meetings, important dates, and deadlines, always with impeccable excuses at hand. If this behavior repeats often enough, your irritation will increase, but if you try to confront them, they very well might try to turn the tables by making you seem uptight and unsympathetic.

You must understand that at the root of this is the

need to make it clear to themselves and to you that they are in some way superior. You must pay attention to the pattern more than the apologies, but also notice the non-verbal signs as they excuse themselves. The tone of the voice is whiny, as if they really feel it is your problem. The apologies are laid on extra thick to disguise the lack of sincerity; in the end, such excuses communicate more about their problems in life than about the facts of their forgetfulness. They are not really sorry.

If this is chronic behavior, you must not get angry or display overt irritation—passive aggressors thrive on getting a rise out of you. Instead, stay calm and subtly mirror their behavior, calling attention to what they are doing, and inducing some shame if possible. You might make dates or appointments and leave them in the lurch, or show up impossibly late with the sincerest of apologies, laced with a touch of irony.

If you are dealing with a boss or someone in a position of power who makes you wait, their assertion of superiority is not so subtle. The best you can do is keep as calm as possible, showing your own form of superiority by remaining patient and cool.

The Sympathy Strategy: Somehow the person you are dealing with is always the victim—of irrational hostility, of unfair circumstances, of society in general. You notice with these types that they seem to relish the drama in their stories. No one else suffers as they do.

As part of this, passive aggressors may display various symptoms and ailments—anxiety attacks, depression, headaches—that make their suffering seem quite real. Since childhood, we have all been capable of willing such symptoms to get attention and sympathy. What you are looking for is the pattern: this seems to recur in passive aggressors when they need something (such as a favor), when they feel you pulling away, when they feel particularly insecure. In any case, they tend to soak up your time and mental space, infecting you with their negative energy and needs, and it is very hard to disengage.

These types will often prey upon those who are prone to feel guilty—the sensitive, caregiving types. To deal with the manipulation involved here you need some distance, and this is not easy. The only way to do this is to feel some anger and resentment at the time and energy you are wasting in trying to help them, and how little they give back to you.

The Dependency Strategy: You are suddenly befriended by someone who is unusually attentive and concerned for your welfare. They want to help you with your work or some other tasks. But every now and then you detect some coldness on their part, and you rack your brain to figure out what you might have said or done to trigger this. In fact, you can't really be sure if they're upset with you, but you find yourself trying to please them nonetheless, and slowly, without really noticing it, the dynamic is reversed, and the displays of sympathy and concern seem to shift from them to you.

This strategy is all about gaining power over

another. You must be wary of those who are too soclitious too early on in a relationship. It is unnatural, as we are normally a bit suspicious of people in the beginning of any relationship. They may be trying to make you dependent in some way, and so you must keep some distance before you can truly gauge their motives. If they start to turn cold and you are confused as to what you did, you can be nearly certain they are using this strategy.

In general, be wary about people's promises and never completely rely on them. With those who fail to deliver, it is more likely a pattern, and it is best to have nothing more to do with them.

The Insinuating-Doubt Strategy: In the course of a conversation, someone you know, perhaps a friend, lets slip a comment that makes you wonder about yourself and if they are in some way insulting you. Perhaps they commend you on your latest work, and with a faint smile they say they imagine you will get lots of attention for it, or lots of money, the implication being that that was your somewhat dubious motive. Or they seem to damn you with faint praise: "You did quite well for someone of your background."

The point of this strategy is to make you feel bad in a way that gets under your skin and causes you to think of the insinuation for days. They want to strike blows at your self-esteem. Most often they are operating out of envy. The best counter is to show that their insinuations have no effect on you. You remain calm. You "agree" with their faint praise and perhaps you return it in kind.

They want to get a rise out of you, and you will not give them this pleasure. Hinting that you might see through them will perhaps infect them with their own doubts, a lesson worth delivering.

The Blame-Shifter Strategy: With certain people, you feel irritated and upset by something they have done. Even before you express your annoyance, they seem to have picked up your mood, and you can detect some sulking on their part. And when you do confront them, they grow silent, wearing a hurt or disappointed look. Any apologies on their part are said in a way (through tone of voice or facial expressions) that subtly conveys some disbelief that they have done anything wrong.

Whatever their type of response, you are left with the feeling that perhaps you were wrong all along. Maybe you overreacted or were paranoid. Now you are the one to feel guilty, as if you were to blame for the tension.

This strategy is a way of covering up all kinds of unpleasant behavior, of deflecting any kind of criticism, and of making people skittish about ever calling them on what they are doing.

To counter this strategy, you need to be able to see through the blame shifting and remain unaffected by it. Your goal is not to make them angry, so don't get caught in the trap of exchanging recriminations. Be calm and even fair, accepting some of the blame for the problem, if that seems right.

What you want is to have the requisite distance to see through them and to disengage. To help in this, you must learn to trust your past feelings. In the moments they are irritating you, write down what they are doing and memorialize their behavior. Perhaps in doing so, you will realize that you are in fact overreacting. But if not, you can return to these notes to convince yourself that you are not crazy and to stop the blame-shifting mechanism in its tracks. If you don't allow the shifting to occur, they might be discouraged from using this strategy. If not, it is best to lessen your involvement with such a passive aggressor.

The Passive-Tyrant Strategy: The person you are working for seems to be bubbling with energy, ideas, and charisma. They are a bit disorganized, but that is normal—they have so much to do, so much responsibility and so many plans, they can't keep on top of it all. They need your help, and you strain every fiber of your being to provide it. Occasionally they praise you, and this keeps you going, but sometimes they rail at you for letting them down, and this sticks in your mind more than the praise.

This strategy is generally used by those in power on their underlings, but it could be applied by people in relationships, one partner tyrannizing the other by simply being impossible to please.

It is very hard to strategize against such types, because most often they are your superiors and have real power over you. The only real counter is to quit and recuperate.

Controlled Aggression

The problem has never been that we humans are assertive and aggressive. The real problem is that we do not know how to harness this energy in an adult, productive, and prosocial manner. This energy needs to be embraced as totally human and potentially positive. Instead of being chronically aggressive, passive-aggressive, or repressed, we can make this energy focused and rational.

The following are four potentially positive elements of this energy that we can discipline and use, improving what evolution has bestowed on us.

Ambition: To say you're ambitious in the world today is often to admit to something slightly dirty, perhaps revealing too much self-absorption. But think back to your childhood and youth—you inevitably entertained big dreams and ambitions for yourself. Embrace that childish part of you, revisit your earliest ambitions, adapt them to your current reality, and make them as specific as possible.

Persistence: If you observe infants, you will notice how willful and relentless they are when they want something. Such persistence is natural to us, but it is a quality that we tend to lose as we get older and our self-confidence fades. This ever-so-slight diminishment in self-belief translates into a reduction in the energy with which we attack the problem.

What you must understand is the following: almost nothing in the world can resist persistent human energy. The trick is to want something badly enough that nothing will stop you or dull your energy. Drop the background doubts and continue striking with full force, knowing that you can break through anything if you don't let up. Once you sense the power in this form of attack, you will keep returning to it.

Fearlessness: We are bold creatures by nature. As children, we were not afraid to ask for more or assert our will. We were remarkably resilient and fearless in so many ways.

You must try to recover the fearlessness you once possessed, through incremental steps. The key is to first convince yourself that you deserve good and better things in life. Once you feel that, you can start by training yourself to speak up or even talk back to people in everyday situations, if they are proving to be insensitive. Once you lose your fear in these less dramatic encounters, you can start to ramp it up. You can make greater demands on people that they treat you well, or honor the quality work that you do. You do this without a complaining or defensive tone.

Anger: What makes anger toxic is the degree to which it is disconnected from reality. People channel their natural frustrations into anger at some vague enemy or scapegoat, conjured up and spread by demagogues. There is no thought behind their anger, and so it leads nowhere or it becomes destructive.

You must do the opposite. Your anger is directed at very specific individuals and forces. You analyze the emotion—are you certain that your frustration does not stem from your own inadequacies? Do you really understand the cause of the anger and what it should be directed at? In addition to determining if it is justified and where the anger should be directed, you also analyze the best way to channel this emotion, the best strategy for defeating your opponents. Your anger is controlled, realistic, and targeted at the actual source of the problem, never losing sight of what initially inspired the emotion.

> Power is required for communication. To stand
> before an indifferent or hostile group and
> have one's say, or to speak honestly to a friend
> truths that go deep and hurt, these require self-
> affirmation, self-assertion, and even at times
> aggression.
>
> —*Rollo May*

17

Seize the Historical Moment

—— ✦ ——

The Law of Generational Myopia

You are born into a generation that defines who you are more than you can imagine. Your generation wants to separate itself from the previous one and set a new tone for the world. In the process, it forms certain tastes, values, and ways of thinking that you as an individual internalize. As you get older, these generational values and ideas tend to close you off from other points of view, constraining your mind. Your task is to understand as deeply as possible this powerful influence on who you are and how you see the world. Knowing in depth the spirit of your generation and the times you live in, you will be better able to exploit the zeitgeist. You will be the one to anticipate and set the trends that your generation hungers for. You will free your mind from the mental constraints placed on you by your generation, and you will become more of the individual you imagine yourself to be, with all the power that freedom will bring you.

Our era is a birth-time, and a period of transition.
The spirit of man has broken with the old order of
things ... and with the old ways of thinking, and is

of the mind to let them all sink into the depths of the past and to set about its own transformation ... The frivolity and boredom which unsettle the established order, the vague foreboding of something unknown, these are the heralds of approaching change.

−G.W.F. Hegel

Keys to Human Nature

Many of us intuit the truth about generations—how they tend to have a kind of personality and how the younger generation initiates so many changes. Some of us are in denial about the phenomenon because we like to imagine that we as individuals shape what we think and believe, or that other forces such as class, gender, and race play a greater role. Certainly the study of generations can be imprecise; it is a subtle and elusive subjective. And other factors play a role as well. But looking in depth at the phenomenon reveals that in fact it is more of an influence than we generally imagine, and is in many ways the great generator of so much that happens in history.

And understanding this generational phenomenon can yield several other benefits: We can see what forces shaped our parents' mind-set, and then ours in turn, as we have tried to go in a different direction. We can make better sense of the underlying changes going on in all areas of society and begin to surmise where the world is headed, to anticipate future trends, and to understand the role we can play in shaping events. This can not only bring us great social power but can also have a therapeutic, calming effect on us as we view events in the world with some distance and equanimity, elevated above the chaotic changes of the moment.

We shall call this knowledge *generational awareness*. To attain it, first we must understand the actual profound effect that our generation has on how we view the world, and second we must understand the larger generational patterns that shape history and recognize where our time period fits into the overall scheme.

The Generational Phenomenon

In the first phase of life, we shape a generational perspective. It is a kind of collective mind-set, as we absorb the prevailing culture at the same time as our peers, from the point of view of childhood and youth. And because we are too young to understand or analyze this perspective, we are generally ignorant of its formation and how it influences what we see and how we interpret events.

Then, when we reach our twenties and into our thirties, we enter a new phase of life and experience a shift. Now we are in a position to assume some power, to actually alter this world according to our own values and ideals. We inevitably clash with the older generation that has held power for some time, as they insist on their own way of acting and evaluating events. Many of them often view us as immature, unsophisticated, soft, undisciplined, pampered, unenlightened, and certainly not ready to assume power.

Then, as we enter our forties and midlife and assume many of the leadership positions in society, we begin to take notice of a younger generation that is fighting for its own power and position. Its members are now judging us and finding our own style and ideas rather irrelevant. We begin to judge them in return, describing them as immature, unsophisticated, soft, et cetera.

When it comes to the changes generated by the tensions between two generations, we can say that the greater part of them will come from the young. They are more restless, in search of their own identity, and more attuned to the group and how they fit in. By the time such a younger generation emerges into their thirties and forties, they will have shaped the world with their changes and given it a look and feel that is distinct from their parents.

The generational mind-set inevitably dominates everyone from within, no matter how they personally try to react against it. We cannot step outside the historical moment that we are born into.

In considering this mind-set, we must try to think in terms of a collective personality, or what we shall call *spirit*. Our generation has inherited from our parents and the past certain key values and ways of looking at the world that remain unquestioned. But at any moment, people of a new generation are searching for something more alive and relevant, something that expresses what is different, what is altering in the present. This sense of what is moving and evolving in the present, as opposed to what is inherited from the past, is the *collective spirit* itself, its restless and searching nature. It is not something we can easily put into words. It is more a mood, an emotional tone, a way that people relate to one another.

If our generation has a particular spirit to it, we could say the same for the time period that we are living through, which generally comprises four generations alive at the same time. The blending of these generations, the tension among them, and the clashing that often occurs create what we shall call the overall spirit of the times or what is commonly known as the zeitgeist.

To see this in your own experience, look back at periods in the past in which you were alive and conscious, at least some twenty years ago, if you are old enough. With some distance, you can reflect upon how different those times felt, what was in the air, how people interacted, the degree of tension. The spirit of that period is not only in the styles and clothes that are different from those of the present, but also in something social and collective, an overall mood or feeling in the air.

Generational Patterns

Since the beginning of recorded time, certain writers and thinkers have intuited a pattern to human history. It was perhaps the great fourteenth-century Islamic scholar Ibn Khaldun who first formulated this idea into the theory that history seems to move in four acts, corresponding to four generations.

The first generation is that of the revolutionaries who make a radical break with the past, establishing new values but also creating some chaos in the struggle to do so. Then along comes a second generation that craves some order.

Those of the third generation—having little direct connection to the founders of the revolution—feel less passionate about it. They are not so interested in ideas but rather in building things.

Along comes the fourth generation, which feels that society has lost its vitality, but they are not sure what should replace it. They begin to question the values they have inherited, some becoming quite cynical. A crisis of sorts emerges. Then comes the revolutionary generation, which, unified around some new belief, finally tears down the old order, and the cycle continues.

Although this pattern certainly has variation and is not a science, we tend to see a lot of the overall sequencing in history.

We can deduce two important lessons from this: First, our values will often depend upon where we fall in this pattern and how our generation reacts against the particular imbalances of the previous generation. Second, we notice that generations seem capable only of reacting and moving in an opposing direction to the previous generation.

In seeing this historical pattern, we must recognize what seems to be an overall human spirit that transcends any particular time and that keeps us evolving. If for any reason the cycle stopped, we would be doomed.

Your task as a student of human nature is threefold: First and foremost, you must alter your attitude toward your own generation. Your goal is to understand as deeply as possible how profoundly the spirit of your generation, and the times that you live in, have influenced how you perceive the world.

Your second task is to create a kind of personality profile of your generation, so that you can understand its spirit in the present and exploit it. What you are looking for is common traits that signal an overall spirit.

You can begin this by looking at the decisive events that occurred in the years before you entered the work world and that played a large role in shaping this personality. For instance, for those who came of age during the 1930s, there was the Depression and then the advent of World War II. You must also factor into this equation any major technological advances or inventions that alter how people interact.

In filling out this profile, look at the parenting styles of those who raised you—permissive, overcontrolling, neglectful, or empathetic. The famously permissive style of those who raised children in the 1890s helped create the wild, carefree attitude of the lost generation of the 1920s.

Like an individual, any generation will tend to have an unconscious, shadow side to its personality. A good sign of this can be found in the particular style of humor that each generation tends to forge. A generation might seem rather prudish and correct, but its humor is raunchy and irreverent. This is the shadow side leaking out.

Your third task, then, is to expand this knowledge to something broader, first trying to piece together what could be considered the zeitgeist. In this sense, you are looking particularly at the relationship between the two dominant generations, early adults (ages twenty-two to forty-four) and those in midlife (forty-five to sixty-six). No matter how close the parents and children of these generations might seem, there is always an underlying tension, along with some resentment and envy. You want to examine this tension and determine which generation tends to dominate and how this power dynamic might be shifting in the present.

This overall awareness will yield several important benefits. For instance, your generational perspective tends to create a particular kind of myopia. Each generation tends toward some imbalance as it reacts to the previous one. There is much to be gained by looking at the world from the perspective of your parents or your children, and even adopting some of their values. You awareness will free you from these mental blocks and illusions, making your mind more fluid and creative.

Strategies for Exploiting the Spirit of the Times

To make the most of the zeitgeist, you must begin with a simple premise: you are a product of the times as much as anyone; the generation you were born into has shaped your thoughts and values, whether you are aware of this or not. And so, if you feel from deep within some frustration with the way things are in the world or with the older generation, or if you sense there is something that is missing in the culture, you can be almost certain that other people of your generation are feeling the same way. And if you are the one to act on this feeling, your work will resonate with your generation and help shape the zeitgeist. With this in mind, you must put into practice some or all of the following strategies.

Push against the past. You may feel a deep need to create something new and more relevant to your generation, but the past will almost always exercise a strong pull on you, in the form of the values of your parents that you internalized at a young age. Because of this, you might hesitate to go full throttle with whatever you do or express, and your defiance of the past ways of doing things will tend to be rather tepid.

Instead you must force yourself in the opposite direction. Use the past and its values or ideas as something to push against with great force, using any anger you might feel to help in this.

Adapt the past to the present spirit. Once you identify the essence of the zeitgeist, it is often a wise strategy to find some analogous moment or period in history. The frustrations and rebellions of your generation were certainly felt to some degree by some previous generation and were expressed in dramatic fashion. You take some of the emotionally loaded symbols and styles of that historical period and adapt them, giving the impression that what you are attempting in the present is a more perfect and progressive version of what happened in the past.

Resurrect the spirit of childhood. By bringing to life the spirit of your early years—its humor, its decisive historical events, the styles and products of the period, the feeling in the air as it affected you—you will reach a vast audience of all those who experienced those years in a similar way. You must use this strategy only if you feel a particularly powerful connection to your childhood.

Keep in mind that you are not aiming for a literal re-creation of the past but capturing its spirit. To have real power, it should connect to some issue or problem in the present and not simply be some mindless bit of nostalgia.

Create the new social configuration. It is human nature for people to crave more social interaction with those with whom they feel an affinity. You will always gain great power by forging some new way of interacting that appeals to your generation. You organize a group around new ideas or values that are in the air or the latest technology that allows you to bring people together of a like mind in a novel way. In this new form of a group, it is always wise to introduce some rituals that bond the members together and some symbols to identify with.

In using this strategy, think of the repressive elements of the past that people are yearning to shake free of. The group you establish will let flourish a new spirit and even offer the thrill of breaking past taboos on correctness.

Subvert the spirit. You might find yourself at odds with some part of the spirit of your generation or the times you live in. Whatever the reason, it is never wise to preach or moralize or condemn the spirit of the times. You will only marginalize yourself. If the spirit of the times is like a tide or a stream, better to find a way to gently redirect it, instead of fighting its direction. You will have more power and effect by working within the zeitgeist and subverting it.

For instance, you make something—a book, a film, any product—that has the look and feel of the times, even to an exaggerated degree. However, through the content of what you produce, you insert ideas and a spirit that is somewhat different, that points to the value of the past you prefer.

Keep adapting. It was in your youth that your generation forged its particular spirit, a period of emotional intensity that we often remember fondly. The problem that you face is that as you get older, you tend to re-main locked in the values, ideas, and styles that marked this period. What you want is to modernize your spirit, to possibly adopt some of the values and ideas of the younger generation that appeal to you, gaining a new and wider audience by blending your experience and perspective with the changes going on, making yourself into an unusual and appealing hybrid.

The Human Beyond Time and Death

We humans are masters of transforming whatever we get our hands on. But one area seems to defy our trans-formational powers—time itself. We are born and enter the stream of life, and each day it carries us closer to death. Time is linear, always advancing, and there is nothing we can do to stop its course.

If we look more closely, however, at our personal experience of time, we can notice something peculiar—the passage of the hours or days can alter depending on our mood and circumstances. A child and an adult ex-perience time very differently—for the former it moves rather slowly, and all too quickly for the latter.

What this means in general is that time is a human creation, a way for us to measure its passage for our own purposes, and our experience of this artificial creation is quite subjective and changeable. Although we cannot stop the aging process or defy the ultimate reality of death, we can alter the experience of them, transforming what is painful and depressing into something much different. We can make time feel more cyclical than linear; we can even step outside the stream and experience forms of timelessness.

Here's how we could apply this active approach to four elemental aspects of time.

The phases of life: As we pass through the phases of life—youth, emerging adult, middle age, and old age—we notice certain common changes in us. In our youth we experience life more intensely. Most of us tend to be outwardly focused, concerned with what people might think of us and with how we fit in.

As we get older, the intensity diminishes, our minds tend to tighten up around certain conventional ideas and beliefs. What we sometimes gain in these later phases is some distance from life, some self-control, and perhaps the wisdom that comes from accumulating experiences.

We have the power, however, to drop or mitigate the negative qualities that often go with certain phases of life, in a way defying the aging process itself. For instance, when we are young, we can make a point of lessening the influence of the group on us and not being so fixated on what others are thinking and doing.

As we age, we can strive to retain the positive youthful qualities that often fade with the years. For instance, we can regain some of the natural curiosity we had as children by dropping some of the smugness and know-it-all attitude that often come over us as we get older.

Present generations: Your goal here is to be *less* a product of the times and to gain the ability to transform your relationship to your generation. A key way of doing this is through active associations with people of different generations. If you are younger, you try to interact more with those of older generations.

If you are older, you reverse this by actively interacting with those of a younger generation, not as a parent or authority figure but as a peer. You allow yourself to absorb their spirit, their different way of thinking, and their enthusiasm.

In interacting on a more authentic level with those of different generations, you are creating a unique bond—that of people alive at the same time in history. This will only enhance your grasp of the zeitgeist.

Past generations: When we think about history, we tend to render the past into a kind of dead and spiritless caricature. Perhaps we feel smug and superior to past eras, and so we focus on those aspects of history that indicate backward ideas and values (not realizing that future generations will do the same to us), seeing what we want to see.

We must rid ourselves of such absurd notions and habits. We are not as superior to those in the past as we like to imagine. Although human nature remains a constant, those in the past faced different circumstances with different levels of technology and had values and beliefs quite different from our own, and not necessarily inferior.

Most important of all, however, we must understand that the past is by no means dead. So many ways we relate to the world now came from changes in thinking long ago.

You must radically alter your own relationship to history, bringing it back to life within you. Begin by taking some era in the past, one that particularly excites you for whatever reason. Try to re-create the spirit of those times, to get inside the subjective experience of the actors you are reading about, using your active imagination. See the world through their eyes. Make use of the excellent books written in the last hundred years to help you gain a feel for daily life in particular periods. In the literature of the time you can detect the prevailing spirit. Drop any tendencies to judge or moralize. People were experiencing their present moment within a context that made sense to them. You want to understand that from the inside out.

In this way you will feel differently about yourself. Your concept of time will expand and you will realize that if the past lives on in you, what you are doing today, the world you live in, will live on and affect the future, connecting you to the larger human spirit that moves through us all.

The future: We can understand our effect on the future most clearly in our relationship to our children, or to those young people we influence in some ways as teachers or mentors. This influence will last years after we are gone. But our work, what we create and contribute to society, can exert even greater power and can become part of a conscious strategy to communicate with those of the future and influence them. Thinking in this way can actually alter what we say or what we do.

> A man's shortcomings are taken from his epoch;
> his virtues and greatness belong to himself.
>
> —*Johann Wolfgang von Goethe*

Meditate on Our Common Mortality

—— ✧ ——

The Law of Death Denial

Most of us spend our lives avoiding the thought of death. Instead, the inevitability of death should be continually on our minds. Understanding the shortness of life fills us with a sense of purpose and urgency to realize our goals. Training ourselves to confront and accept this reality makes it easier to manage the inevitable setbacks, separations, and crises in life. It gives us a sense of proportion, of what really matters in this brief existence of ours. Most people continually look for ways to separate themselves from others and feel superior. Instead, we must see the mortality in everyone, how it equalizes and connects us all. By becoming deeply aware of our mortality, we intensify our experience of every aspect of life.

When I look back at the past and think of all the time I squandered in error and idleness, lacking the knowledge needed to live, when I think of how often I sinned against my heart and my soul, then my heart bleeds. Life is a gift, life is happiness, every minute could have been an eternity of

happiness! If youth only knew! Now my life will
change; now I will be reborn. Dear brother, I swear
that I shall not lose hope. I will keep my soul pure
and my heart open. I will be reborn for the better.

—Fyodor Dostoyevsky

Keys to Human Nature

For us humans, death is a source not only of fear but
also of awkwardness. We are the only animal truly conscious of our impending mortality. In general, we owe
our power as a species to our ability to think and reflect. But in this particular case, our thinking brings us
nothing but misery. All we can see is the physical pain
involved in dying, the separation from loved ones, and
the uncertainty as to when such a moment might arrive.
We do what we can to avoid the thought, to distract ourselves from the reality, but the awareness of death lies
in the back of our minds and can never be completely
shaken.

We became aware of our mortality quite early on
in childhood, and this filled us with an anxiety that we
cannot remember but that was very real and visceral.
Such anxiety cannot be wished away or denied. It sits in
us as adults in a powerful latent form. When we choose
to repress the thought of death, our anxiety is only made
stronger by our not confronting the source of it. The
slightest incident or uncertainty about the future will
tend to stir up this anxiety and even make it chronic.

To fight this, we will tend to narrow down the scope of our thoughts and activities; if we don't leave our comfort zones in what we think and do, then we can make life rather predictable and feel less vulnerable to anxiety. Certain addictions to foods or stimulants or forms of entertainment will have a similar dulling effect.

If we take this far enough, we become increasingly self-absorbed and less dependent on people, who often stir up our anxieties with their unpredictable behavior.

We can describe the contrast between life and death in the following manner: Death is absolute stillness, without movement or change except decay. In death we are separated from others and completely alone. Life on the other hand is movement, connection to other living things, and diversity of life forms. By denying and repressing the thought of death, we feed our anxieties and become more deathlike from within—separated from other people, our thinking habitual and repetitive, with little overall movement and change. On the other hand, the familiarity and closeness with death, the ability to confront the thought of it has the paradoxical effect of making us feel more alive.

By connecting to the reality of death, we connect more profoundly to the reality and fullness of life. By separating death from life and repressing our awareness of it, we do the opposite.

What we require in the modern world is a way to create for ourselves the positive paradoxical effect. The following is an attempt to help accomplish this, by forging a practical philosophy for transforming the consciousness of our mortality into something productive and life enhancing.

A Philosophy of Life Through Death

The philosophy we are adopting depends on our ability to go in the opposite direction we normally feel toward death—to look at it more closely and deeply.

The following are five key strategies, with appropriate exercises, to help us achieve this. It is best to put all five into practice, so that this philosophy can seep into our daily consciousness and alter our experience from within.

Make the awareness visceral. Normally we go through life in a very distracted, dreamlike state, with our gaze turned inward. Much of our mental activity revolves around fantasies and resentments that are completely internal and have little relationship to reality. The proximity of death suddenly snaps us to attention as our whole body responds to the threat. We feel the rush of adrenaline, the blood pumping extra hard to the brain and through the nervous system. This focuses the mind to a much higher level and we notice new details, see people's faces in a new light, and sense the impermanence in everything around us, deepening our emotional responses. This effect can linger for years, even decades.

We cannot reproduce that experience without

risking our lives, but we can gain some of the effect through smaller doses. We must begin by meditating on our death and seeking to convert it into something more real and physical. We can often sense death's physicality in those moments before we fall asleep—for a few seconds we feel ourselves passing from one form of consciousness to another, and that slip has a deathlike sensation. There is nothing to be afraid of in this; in fact, in moving in this direction, we make major advancements in diminishing our chronic anxiety.

We can use our imagination in this as well, by envisioning the day our death arrives, where we might be, how it might come. We can also try to look at the world as if we were seeing things for the last time—the people around us, the everyday sights and sounds, the hum of the traffic, the sound of the birds, the view outside our window.

We must not be afraid of the pangs of sadness that ensue from this perception. The tightness of our emotions, usually so wound up around our own needs and concerns, is now opening up to the world and to the poignancy of life itself, and we should welcome this.

Awaken to the shortness of life. When we unconsciously disconnect ourselves from the awareness of death, we forge a particular relationship to time—one that is rather loose and distended. We come to imagine that we always have more time than is the reality.

Then, if a deadline is forced upon us on a particular project, that dream-like relationship to time is shattered and for some mysterious reason we find the focus to get done in days what would have taken weeks or months. The change imposed upon us by the deadline has a physical component: our adrenaline is pumping, filling us with energy and concentrating the mind, making it more creative.

We must think of our mortality as a kind of continual deadline, giving a similar effect as described above to all our actions in life. We must stop fooling ourselves: we could die tomorrow, and even if we live for another eighty years, it is but a drop in the ocean of the vastness of time, and it passes always more quickly than we imagine.

Let the awareness of the shortness of life clarify our daily actions. We have goals to reach, projects to get done, relationships to improve. This could be our last such project, our last battle on earth, given the uncertainties of life, and we must commit completely to what we do.

See the mortality in everyone. In 1665 a terrible plague roared through London, killing close to 100,000 inhabitants. The writer Daniel Defoe was only five years old at the time, but he witnessed the plague firsthand and it left a lasting impression on him. Some sixty years later, he decided to re-create the events in London that year through the eyes of an older narrator, using his own memories, much research, and the journal of his uncle, creating the book *A Journal of the Plague Year.*

As the plague raged, the narrator of the book

notices a peculiar phenomenon: people tend to feel much greater levels of empathy toward their fellow Londoners; the normal differences between them, particularly over religious issues, vanish.

With the plague, no one is spared, no matter their wealth or station in life. Feeling personally vulnerable and seeing the vulnerability of everyone else, people's normal sense of difference and privilege is melted away, and an uncommon generalized empathy emerges.

With our philosophy, we want to manufacture the cleansing effect that the plague has on our tribal tendencies and usual self-absorption. We want to begin this on a smaller scale, by looking first at those around us, in our home and our workplace, seeing and imagining their deaths and noting how this can suddenly alter our perception of them. We want to see that uniqueness of the other person in the present, bringing out those qualities we have taken for granted. We want to experience *their* vulnerability to pain and death, not just our own.

We can take this meditation further. Let us look at the pedestrians in any busy city and realize that in ninety years it is likely that none of them will be alive, including us.

The more we can create this visceral connection to people through our common mortality, the better we are able to handle human nature in all its varieties with tolerance and grace.

Embrace all pain and diversity. There is much in life we cannot control, with death as the ultimate example of this. We will experience illness and physical pain. We will go through separation with people. We will face failures from our own mistakes and the nasty malevolence of our fellow humans. And our task is to accept these moments, and even embrace them, not for the pain but for the opportunities to learn and strengthen ourselves. In doing so, we affirm life itself, accepting all of its possibilities. And at the core of this is our complete acceptance of death.

We put this into practice by continually seeing events as fateful—everything happens for a reason, and it is up to us to glean the lesson.

This love of fate has the power to alter everything we experience and lighten the burdens we carry. Why complain over this or that, when in fact we see such events as occurring for a reason and ultimately enlightening us? Why feel envy for what others have, when we possess something far greater—the ultimate approach to the harsh realities of life?

Open the mind to the Sublime. Think of death as a kind of threshold we all must cross. As such, it represents the ultimate mystery. We cannot possibly find the words or concepts to express what it is. We confront something that is truly unknowable. No amount of science or technology or expertise can solve this riddle or verbalize it. We humans can fool ourselves that we know just about everything, but at this threshold we are finally left dumb and groping.

This confrontation with something we cannot know

or verbalize is what we shall call the *Sublime*, whose Latin root means "up to the threshold." The Sublime is anything that exceeds our capacity for words or concepts by being too large, too vast, too dark and mysterious. And when we face such things, we feel a touch of fear but also awe and wonder. We are reminded of our smallness, of what is much vaster and more powerful than our puny will. Feeling the Sublime is the perfect antidote to our complacency and to the petty concerns of daily life that can consume us and leave us feeling rather empty.

The model for feeling the Sublime comes in our meditation on mortality, but we can train our minds to experience it through other thoughts and actions. For instance, when we look up at the night sky, we can let our minds try to fathom the infinity of space and the overwhelming smallness of our planet, lost in all the darkness.

We can experience the Sublime by contemplating other forms of life. We have our own belief about what is real based on our nervous and perceptual systems, but the reality of bats, which perceive through echolocation, is of a different order. They sense things beyond our perceptual system. What are the other elements we cannot perceive, the other realities invisible to us?

We can also expose ourselves to places on the planet where all our normal compass points are scrambled—a vastly different culture or certain landscapes where the human element seems particularly puny, such as the open sea, a vast expanse of snow, a particularly enormous mountain. Physically confronted with what dwarfs us, we are forced to reverse our normal perception, in which we are the center and measure of everything.

In the face of the Sublime, we feel a shiver, a foretaste of death itself, something too large for our minds to encompass. And for a moment it shakes us out of our smugness and releases us from the deathlike grip of habit and banality.

In the end, think of this philosophy in the following terms: Since the beginning of human consciousness, our awareness of death has terrified us. This terror has shaped our beliefs, our religions, our institutions, and so much of our behavior in ways we cannot see or understand. We humans have become the slaves to our fears and our evasions.

When we turn this around, becoming more aware of our mortality, we experience a taste of true freedom. We no longer feel the need to restrict what we think and do, in order to make life predictable. We can be more daring without feeling afraid of the consequences. We can cut loose from all the illusions and addictions that we employ to numb our anxiety. We can commit fully to our work, to our relationships, to all our actions. And once we experience some of this freedom, we will want to explore further and expand our possibilities as far as time will allow us.

Let us rid death of its strangeness, come to know it, get used to it. Let us have nothing on our minds as often as death. At every moment let us picture it in

our imagination in all its aspects ... It is uncertain
where death awaits us; let us await it everywhere.
Premeditation of death is premeditation of
freedom ... He who has learned how to die has
unlearned how to be a slave. Knowing how to die
frees us from all subjection and constraint.

–Michel de Montaigne